Hair Tells a Story

Hair Tells a Story

Hers, Yours and Ours

Margo Maine

Toplight

Jefferson, North Carolina

ISBN (print) 978-1-4766-8861-9
ISBN (ebook) 978-1-4766-4797-5

Library of Congress and British Library
Cataloguing-in-Publication Data

Library of Congress Control Number 2022056386

Front cover images © Nadia Grapes/Shutterstock

Printed in the United States of America

Toplight is an imprint of McFarland & Company, Inc., Publishers

*Box 611, Jefferson, North Carolina 28640
www.toplightbooks.com*

Contents

Contents

Acknowledgments

First, I must acknowledge that I am one very lucky soul to have had the support system I needed to write this book. Yes, "it takes a village" and I have been blessed with a special village my whole life. My family—especially my parents—lived a life of integrity, perseverance, and hard work: caring for others and making the world a better place were both spoken and unspoken values. What a great beginning.

Over the years, I have enjoyed amazing friends and colleagues, always sticking by my side throughout professional challenges and surviving the eight books I have written. I especially want to thank Carol Dohanyos, Lin Druschel, and Beth McGilley, longtime friends who have been living this dream since I started thinking about hair back in the first Obama administration. Others on this varsity team include Amy Banks, Jessica Baker, Lindsay Cohen, Carmen Cool, Carolyn Costin, Jennifer Gaudiani, Judi Goldstein, the late and dearly missed Lynn Grefe, Lindsey Hall, Beth Harrell, Ann Kearney-Cook, Sondra Kronberg, Martha Levine, Gina MacDonald, Dianne Neumark-Sztainer, Niva Piran, Judy Rabinor, Adrienne Ressler, Karen Samuels, Jenni Schaefer, Meri Shadley, Anita Sinicrope Maier, Joslyn Smith, Mary Tantillo, and Elissa Zelman.

My support team at home includes friends Mary Dineen-Elovich, Kathleen Kay, and my sometimes-running-partner Duby McDowell. Laura Alabre, Kadzo Kangwana, and Mariela Podolski brighten the mood and ambiance of our shared office at Maine & Weinstein Specialty Group. And of course, gratitude goes to my support staff, Kimberly and Beth (Kimberly Boutique), Pamela Rosin (Phillip David Jewelers), and Carol McSheffery (hair stylist) for the pleasure and beauty they bring into my life.

Acknowledgments

I have benefited tremendously from the guidance and instruction of Patricia Bolger, a 14th Generation Emei Qigong master, over the last decade. The practice of Qigong has added immeasurably to my perspective on life.

You may have noticed all the women's names above, but I have an impressive group of male friends and colleagues as well. Rob Weinstein is my "work husband"—we have practiced together for more than 30 years, longer than most marriages. We still have fun despite how challenging our work can be. Along with Rob, I am grateful for the support of Michael Berrett, Ovidio Bermudez, Don Blackwell, Doug Bunnell, Leigh Cohn, Steve Emmett, David Hall, Craig Johnson, Joe Kelly, Michael Levine, Sam Menaged, Mark Warren, and Ken Willis, all of whom are members of the Renfrew Men's Group. (I'm the token female.) Admittedly, I am a female chauvinist, but these men are stalwart supporters of feminism and feminists.

Closer to home is my husband George Coppolo—speaking of a great soul, he is that. The most important qualities in a life partner start with someone who brings out the best in you and makes you laugh. He has been doing both of those for me for a long time now—and I hope I do the same for him. Writing can be a very lonely process, but George's humor and presence, patience, and support, along with his great head of hair, and our two cats Scout and Ziggy, with their luxurious coats, never let me feel alone. Scout spent a lot of time purring on my lap in the final stages of this book but died a few weeks before my deadline. Here's to you, Scout!

Special appreciation to Joe Kelly, Beth McGilley, and Gina MacDonald—all mentioned above—for their reviewing the manuscript and providing editorial ideas and comments on the content. They enriched the book as they always enrich my perspective. And deep gratitude for the friendship and support of Alan Nero, his family and "The Gilson" crew.

Early in the process of writing the book proposal, I had the unique opportunity of working with Christina Baker Kline, *New York Times* bestselling author of eight novels, including *The Exiles*, *Orphan Train*, and *A Piece of the World*. Her editing, consultation, and advice helped immensely.

Acknowledgments

I appreciate the chance to work with Managing Editor Susan Kilby and her staff at McFarland. They have been supportive and helpful from the start and I feel fortunate to have this partnership.

I also need to acknowledge the things that invigorate me every day. I get up early in the morning to watch the sun come up and spend time outside appreciating our Mother Earth. Sunrise stirs my soul and reminds me of the beauty and potential in each precious day. I listen to NPR for information and to the Beatles for inspiration. Life would be lean and mean without their music.

And, finally, endless appreciation for all the women who shared their hair stories with me. I have learned so much and hope they feel well represented in this discussion and empowered to embrace their hair stories and to live fully and freely.

Preface

I write because I listen, and I have been listening to women's stories my whole life. In fact, I have listened so much that *Hair Tells a Story* is my eighth book. To be honest, sometimes I wonder if writing is a compulsion for me: friends have certainly suggested this. Writing takes endless time, dedication, and hard work. It requires giving up other activities that would be a lot easier and light up the pleasure centers of my brain much sooner. (We all love dopamine!) Still, writing seems to be in my DNA. My nature is to try to see connections, to make sense of things, and to help others. Writing channels this energy more effectively for me than anything else I can imagine.

For nearly 40 years now as a clinical psychologist, I have dedicated my career to improving women's lives, specializing in the treatment and prevention of eating disorders and body image issues. Listening to their stories has opened my eyes to so much about today's female experience. The body has truly become the canvas upon which contemporary women paint their secrets and self-doubt, their hopes and their dreams, their pain, and their disappointments. Hair sits right on top, with feelings from deep within our hearts and our histories, showing up for everyone to see. Hair always tells a story.

Hair may tell our stories, but too often pain, anxiety, racism, sexism, and rigid beauty standards underlie these stories. The multi-layered, deep meaning of hair cuts across the boundaries of age, place, ethnicity, race, cultural origins, class, ability, sexual orientation, and gender identification. Yet, little is written about the interplay of the historical, psychological, and social aspects of women's hair. Books about the importance of hair have tended to be highly academic or dated, to speak to small or specialized, but important,

1

audiences, or to mention hair only in passing. The personal psychology and the universal, entangled, and lifelong meaning of hair have been missing. I am hoping to fill this niche, empowering women to understand how the hair on their heads reflects what is deep in their hearts, as well as to acknowledge and address the many sociocultural and relational pressures they have experienced regarding their hair.

This topic is truly timely. As we move through a global pandemic limiting our access to routine hair care services and products, hair has become a metaphor. Many women have felt out of control of key aspects of their lives, with hair unexpectedly becoming a central and critical concern—a virtual hot spot. With so much of both our personal and our professional communication now online, through platforms like Zoom and FaceTime, we never escape what we look like. The iconic "bad hair day" is now a "bad hair year," or two, or more. For some, the silver lining has been to come to terms with natural hair—be that gray or kinky or both—instead of younger or straighter hair. For others, the loss of control over this aspect of appearance has contributed to a greater sense of loss, depression, uncertainty, and anxiety.

And, as "the other pandemic" of racism has birthed a long-needed recognition that Black Lives Matter, we also know that black hair matters. Hair is never just hair.

I began the research and writing process for this book before 2010. Since then, I have been integrating personal and professional observations and experiences with interviews (some in person, some by phone, some by email) with women, from 16 years old to 80-plus, from all over the United States, as well as with hair professionals and writers across the globe. (I have changed the names and identifying information of the women who shared their stories but maintained the sentiment and feelings.) Women have been eager to express what hair means to them, recounting powerful and surprising memories and experiences. Each conversation reinforced the importance of completing this project and kept me interested, excited, and engaged despite the eternal question of how I would get this written while practicing full-time, writing another book and various professional articles, lecturing frequently at conferences, providing leadership in my field, and trying to educate the world about eating disorders and women's health. The pandemic slowed down my speaking engagements and travel, so I was able to return to this passion. I am thrilled to be able to share these hair stories and help you to understand your own. In this past decade, our collective understanding of the complexity of gender identification has expanded beyond the binary framework. I refer to "women" throughout the book, despite acknowledging the limitations of a singular word to refer to those who identify as female.

Having listened to their struggles for decades now, I appreciate that contemporary women speak through their bodies and that hair can tell deep truths about their lives. An unrecognized element in women's history, it is time to tell the stories and acknowledge the power of hair. This book begins to tell that story.

Introduction

Although countless books and articles address the body image issues of contemporary women, they generally ignore the role of hair—it is the forgotten body part, a body image orphan. Yet, hair has consistently served as a second, nonverbal language to express critical sentiments, telling the story of women's lives like nothing else does.

Every woman has a story about the meaning her hair holds and has held throughout her life. One of the initial images when we look at each other, it is in fact the first thing that others see as a baby is born—and often the first bragging point for parents and grandparents. Hair grows on our heads, the body part we most associate with intellect, spirit, emotion, communication, and individuality. In energy medicine and tantric philosophy, the top of our heads is considered the crown chakra, connecting our individual, unique soul to the universe and to higher levels of spirituality. Our seven chakras are part of the energetic system of the universe—starting with the root to the earth. Hair is a public, external, and shared experience, connected to the earth below and the universe beyond, but simultaneously deeply personal and internal, emerging from our very core. Hair just may be the "mirror to our soul," as one woman described.

As soon as I say I am writing a book about hair, women look at me quizzically, often saying something like "Really—a book about hair?" I have written seven important books on the serious topic of eating disorders, as that is my clinical specialty, so this topic surprises them. Although their instant response is almost dismissive, most seem to have a sudden epiphany and, within seconds, they are telling me a hair story. Running at sunrise, shopping midday, at a holiday party, waiting to be seated at a restaurant and, of course, in "ladies' rooms" across the country—you name the place, and a woman has talked to me about her hair and what it has meant to her.

Men also have "aha" moments when I describe this writing project—soon sharing the emotions they have watched their women friends, partners, mothers, sisters, and daughters experience surrounding their hair. Men often express a deep desire to understand the special significance and multiple meanings of women's hair so they can be supportive. Many are just baffled at why women care so much about it. For most, but not all, men, the subject is simpler, although quite a few have shared later conversations with me revealing new insights about what their hair has meant to them over the years—especially those who are balding. Regardless, when hair is the subject, I always learn something new—and often quite startling—even about people I know intimately, like close friends or longstanding patients.

I approach this subject as a Caucasian American woman living with many advantages and freedoms. For women of other cultures, however, hair may have even more power and meaning. Masih Alinejad, a contemporary Iranian feminist and activist, launched a social movement, My Stealthy Freedom, after realizing how limited women's lives are in Iran. In 2014 she posted a photo on Facebook of herself running down a London street, head uncovered, with the wind in her hair, experiencing the liberation of an act that I have always taken for granted. Alinejad resents that part of her body had "been hijacked and replaced with a head scarf,"[1] asserting that if a woman cannot control what covers her head, she cannot control what goes on inside that head. Before long, Alinejad had more than a million followers on Facebook and women began to send her images of themselves without the compulsory hijab covering their hair and limiting the freedoms available to the boys and men around them.

All Alinejad wants is for women to be able to make the decision to cover their heads, or not, independently. Her activism on this and other political issues in Iran has led to her being arrested many times, her family members being detained, and severe travel restrictions. As she has said, "I've got too much hair, too much voice and I'm too much of a woman for them."[2]

Simply by showing their hair, women in repressive cultures can challenge the oppression and the denial of their basic human rights. Hair has power. It is time we understand it.

Hair Tells a Story begins this discussion, integrating sociological, historical, and psychological perspectives about hair. Blending my professional interactions with patients and colleagues in the field of body image and eating disorders, with interviews of women willing to talk about what their hair has meant over their lives, and with hair stylists, I understand that hair is never just hair. Instead, it is an unrecognized element in women's history, revealing much about our legal, social, and psychological status. The "right to choose" is not just about reproductive freedom after all. Expressing ourselves through our hair is a basic human right. Hair matters.

Hair Matters:
Untangling the Universal and Unique

CHAPTER 1

Every Woman's Issue

"Quietly and unexpectedly, hair has become our court of deliberation, the place where we contemplate who and what we are."—Grant McCracken[1]

For most women today, hair is central to self-image and it can be managed, altered, or "improved" quite easily—unlike most body parts. No woman can instantly change her thighs, stomach, or derriere (the most common targets of women's body ambivalence or outright body hatred) the way a quick cut, color, or curl can transform the hair on her head. In fact, between the pandemic and today's tough economic times, hair may take on even greater importance as many women have less expendable income for clothing and fashion. A box of hair color or a new style costs far less than a whole new outfit. As one woman advised: "If you have to pick between a good haircut and a new dress, pick the hair."

Cultural anthropologists Nancy Scheper-Hughes and Margaret Lock (1987)[2] conceptualize the body as composed of three interrelating bodies: the individual, the social, and the political. The individual lived experience of the "body-self" and the use of the body to symbolize or represent social messages take place within a greater political system that regulates, watches, and controls our bodies. More malleable than other body parts and often the first feature others notice, hair occupies a special role in the "body-self" and in the lives of women. Thus, although a woman's *hair-story* is *her* uniquely nuanced story, it is also tempered by the meaning our culture places on women in general and on that woman in particular—the social and political body self. Hair visibly expresses many things about themselves: ties to the past, to their families, to their ethnicity, race,

11

and culture; and breaks with such traditions through radical changes of appearance, either adhering to or rejecting the current trends.

Constraint and Control

Today we often focus on hair as a personal statement, but it has long been a means of social constraint, reflecting the belief that women must be controlled and not be trusted to make their own decisions, even about the length of their hair. Over and over, hair has symbolized a kind of power that could not be trusted. Controlling women's hair has been a way to constrict their spirit, their sexuality, and their autonomy.

Although associated with the Islam religion, the veiling of women predates the founding of Islam. Starting as far back as the 4th century, the Catholic Church issued religious decrees prohibiting women from cutting their hair, threatening excommunication. Later, in medieval Europe, women's heads were covered "to keep their desire in check."[3] In the early colonial days in the United States, laws in some states ordered that a woman's hair belonged to her husband—a wife could not cut it without his permission.[4]

As recently as a century ago, in the early 1900s, American women were expected to cover their hair with a hat, scarf, or veil whenever they were out of their homes, not just when they were in church.[5] Those who refused to comply were judged harshly and seen as deviant or immoral. This remains the belief in many conservative cultures today. Women have struggled to escape their status as second-class citizens and to assert their own authority: hair continues to play a central role in the battles for power and control of women's lives.

Hair also tells an emotional story, often one of personal growth and transformation. In many cultures, passages from childhood to adolescence or adolescence to adulthood are marked by changes in hairstyle. In some African tribes, hair is cut or shaved, signifying each new life stage, communicating marital status through the specific ways a woman's hair is braided and culminating with being shaved for the final time after death.[6] Upper caste Hindu wives wear their hair long and tightly braided, but if they are widowed, the head is shaved and is to remain shaven, indicating that their sexual life is over. In orthodox Jewish traditions, women's heads were often shaved at marriage and then covered with a wig or cloth.[7] A practice in some Native American cultures is to cut one's hair after a significant loss, especially a death, as if getting rid of hair will get rid of the energy connected to that loss.[8] To this day, when women make a major change in hairstyle, it often reflects a major emotional shift—a deep inner experience which needs some outward representation.

The use of hair as a symbol or a code for unspoken but powerful dynamics is not new. Although physically hair is not itself gendered, most cultures have sexualized hair, making it a potent symbol of sexuality and femininity that needs to be controlled or covered, as seen in fundamentalist religions and groups. When a subject is both universal and deeply personal, we tend not to talk out loud about it, fearful of embarrassing ourselves. Instead, we often maintain an obsessive, sometimes self-critical inner dialogue. It is time to start talking.

"A woman who cuts her hair is about to change her life."
—COCO CHANEL[9]

A Haircut Is Never Just a Haircut

For women, hair is like a Rorschach, the projective expression of who we are, who we have been, and who we want to be. This obvious, external feature often reveals a woman's innermost, and sometimes secret, even unconscious, self, telling the story of our lives like nothing else does. We express ourselves, our mood, our culture, our religion, our ethnicity, our family, our status, our age, sometimes even our politics through it.

A quick glance at our hair in old photos instantly reminds us of what was going on in our lives at that time, from our friendships and romantic relationships to the social and cultural context to our deepest emotional states. For me, as a young woman coming of age in the late 1960s, my long hair broadcast my allegiance to the counterculture, my resistance to the status quo, and my desire to be seen for who I was and what I believed. Today, young people who want to be identified with the goth or punk subcultures use their hair to announce their dissatisfaction with the norms they are expected to follow. Often my patients, regardless of age, come in with a totally different hair color or style, with added extensions, or with streaks of neon or even with every hair shaved away, when amidst a period of crisis or unsettling change. Before they speak, their hair announces that something big is happening inside them and they want the whole world to know.

In all my years of coursework, training, and ongoing education, not to mention the countless books and journals and webinars, I never heard anyone say that a change of hairstyle could be a life-changing, and even a life-threatening, situation. But then a 16-year-old patient taught me what I had never learned in libraries, lecture halls or online forums. Karen was in early recovery from anorexia nervosa. Soon after discharge from the inpatient program for eating disorders that I directed, she was unable to cope after a haircut did not turn out quite as she had expected. Our treatment program had gotten her and her family through some major issues, including severe medical problems secondary to her starvation, so this sudden crisis blindsided me.

Karen had decided that a new hairstyle would alleviate all the anxiety and confusion she felt as she tried to sort out her life and the meaning of her eating disorder, left the safety and security of the hospital, faced eating more normally and being at an average weight, and returned to her home and school. Suddenly immersed in all the typical pressures of a girl's junior year in high school, Karen needed to catch up on schoolwork, re-establish herself with teachers, friends, and activities, and respond to boys who suddenly found her attractive. It was all too much. Although she felt out of control and lost without her eating disorder, it was her hair that sent Karen into panic and despair. Her mother called my office for an emergency appointment, reporting that Karen was so anxious and agitated that they could not wait for the scheduled time later that week. When she arrived, Karen was in a panic and could barely sit down. Pacing around my office, she tearfully described how disappointed and shaken she was by her hair and said she was contemplating suicide.

Fortunately, her parents had taken her seriously, because Karen truly could not cope with these overwhelming feelings of despair—she could not imagine living with her hair as it now looked. She had wanted some other new image that she could not quite define but now she wanted to die and had been thinking of methods and how and when she would end her life. Her parents agreed with my recommendation that she be re-admitted to our program for several days to provide a safe environment where she could verbalize and address all the stressors she faced, without hurting herself or reverting to her eating disorder behaviors to numb her pain and confusion.

Once she was able to talk more about the difficulties of her transition back to school and to the new reality of having feelings no longer numbed by her eating disorder, Karen was able to entertain my suggestion that her hair was a fixable problem. We talked about slowing down her expectations about her re-entry into school and social life, helped her parents to understand what support she needed from them, and explored what she really wanted when she had changed that hairstyle. She had thought a new look would instantly make her feel confident, attractive, and capable, ready to be the girl she wanted to be and believed others expected. She left the hospital stronger and clearer, and, with her mother's support, returned to the hair salon for a re-do that helped her feel more in control.

Since that day with Karen and her worried family, I have encountered many women—not just my patients—who have become despondent and even suicidal when a new hairstyle or color disappoints them. Hair stylists regularly encounter these emotional crises with clients who are searching for more than what a new look can bring them. Despite their strengths and achievements, countless women struggle with their hair, spending endless hours on it each week, never really liking the result. Their hair cannot quite deliver the peace of mind, self-confidence, or statement that they want.

Karen's experience taught me so much about what hair can

mean to women, especially when we are at vulnerable points in our lives. Her hairstylist was sensitive and responsive to Karen's emotional state and was instrumental in helping her through this transitional time as she recovered from her eating disorder and developed a stronger sense of her personal identity. This was an eye-opening and heart-warming experience for me as a clinician. I suddenly recognized how important hairstylists can be when we are feeling uncertain of ourselves, overwhelmed by confusing emotions, or searching for our identity. Since opening my eyes to this, I have witnessed the outpouring of stylists' sensitivity and support help so many women.

From Heart to Head

The top of our heads is so often the mirror for what is deep in our hearts. Hair always tells a story, and we can learn so much about a woman by asking her what her hair means to her. After I had been treating her for four years, a patient truly shocked me when she announced that her great hair is not actually her hair. I thought I knew her inside and out, but I had no clue that her hair was so central to her sense of self and personal power.

Cassandra is a strikingly beautiful woman who turns heads wherever she goes. Despite her fair share of body image issues, she always appears self-confident and proud of her appearance. Over the course of our work together, she faced many challenges: the end of her relationship, the loss of her job in a tumbling economy, a struggle to re-invent herself, and responsibility for an ill and aging parent, not to mention longstanding depression and bulimia. Cassandra shared so much of herself but never once talked about her hair in any depth (nor did I ask as we had so many other issues to discuss) and her compulsion to cover it up with hair from some other person from some other country. (See Chapter 6 about the hair/wig industries.) Talking about this opened the door to deeper issues that we continued to explore about her heritage, her place in the world as a biracial woman, her femininity, her reliance on her appearance, and more.

One week, an 18-year-old patient came in with black hair instead of her natural light and sunny brown tresses. She had just finished her first semester in college, had done well, but not as well as she expected, had her first real fight with her boyfriend of two years, and was facing her parents' ongoing conflicts and her mother's desire for a separation. In response to these painful issues, Marci wanted her hair to look as dark as her spirits. She did look strikingly different, as she intended—no one who knew her would miss this. Black hair was the only way she knew to show the depth of her sadness and all the other feelings swimming inside her. To communicate her angst, she would wear her heart on her head—not on her sleeve as that old saying suggests. Her family and friends got the message and rallied to support her during this upside down time in her life. At her next appointment, she was feeling stronger and more capable of getting through these unexpected challenges, but she still needed black hair to reveal her complicated emotions. She was contemplating a tattoo to illustrate what she could not express verbally, but her hair was the quickest and easiest way to express her pain.

Despite how much hair means to women, most of the time these feelings just seem to float around, rarely translated into words. My conversations with women about their hair range from women who play with their hair in a celebratory and creative way to those who use it to camouflage serious self-destructive impulses or to manage overwhelming anxiety or self-doubt. Hair speaks, with a voice that is sometimes loud and clear, at other times subtle and subliminal.

Marissa used her hair to reveal the most desperate feelings a woman can have. When I first met her, I saw an attractive 40-something woman with silky, long black hair, but she felt anything but attractive. Although open and engaged from the start of our therapy sessions, Marissa never told me that she had ever been suicidal when I asked standard questions about mood and depression at our first meeting. Months later, when I mentioned that I was writing about women and hair, she volunteered that, as her marriage fell apart, she contemplated killing herself and used her hair to convey her overwhelming anger and grief to the world. Words could not convey her confusion and despair as she faced the inevitable decision whether to divorce an unfaithful husband. She translated her heartbreak and anguish into the language of her hair, first through its color, explaining: "Black is powerful, strong, fierce, frightening. I wanted a change and to send the message that I was not going to let myself be hurt." Later, she punctuated this nonverbal statement through shaving her head and getting rid of her hair entirely.

Marissa acted out powerful self-destructive impulses on her hair. She had small children and, although her suddenly bald head confused them, at least she had found a way to discharge some of her feelings without killing herself and leaving them behind. She taught me that a drastic change of hairstyle could camouflage serious self-destructive impulses and that it might even keep a despondent woman from suicide. Marissa thought seriously about ending her life but expressing all those emotions through her hair gave her some relief and kept her from taking that step. (Read more about Marissa in Chapter 12.)

Since I helped Karen and her family through her suicidal reaction to her hair, my eyes have been opened wide to the powerful role hair has in our lives. Women like Marci and Marissa who drastically change their hair to cope with severe despair and hopelessness illustrate how interconnected the hair on our heads is to the deepest emotional experiences in our hearts. Our hair always tells a story.

CHAPTER 2

Women and Hair:
A Love-Hate Story

"Hair is the western woman's veil."—Arwa Mahdawi[1]

The story about women and their hair is complex—for many, a love-hate relationship. In an era characterized by obsessive concerns about weight, appearance, and beauty, hair can be the ticket to feeling in control of an important symbol of who a woman is, what she values, and what her value is to others. But it also can enslave her, exhausting her energy and self-confidence.

If hair is a problem, life is a problem for many women. Market research tells us a great deal about how women in the United States experience their hair:

- 87% of women describe their hair as a central aspect of their personality.[2]
- 68% say a "bad hair day" affects their self-confidence and impedes their work performance.[3]
- 23% of women do not want to leave their house on a bad hair day.[4]
- 68% of women feel instantly more attractive after having their hair colored.[5]
- Women who felt that they looked younger after a cut, color or both showed a drop in blood pressure according to a Harvard study.[6] Can a haircut make your body healthier?
- By the time a 10-year-old is 50, she may have spent nearly $300,000 on just her hair and face.[7]

Body image and appearance are not just adolescent issues—they start early and have no expiration date. It is bad enough that our culture has oversexualized girls for years but now we are diva-tizing them, engaging them at very young ages in "beauty" mainte-nance and appearance concerns. These little divas are not sneaking their mothers' lipsticks. Instead, they have their own assortment of fancy, flavored lip glosses in their own little makeup kits.

Hair is no exception as we see how much time and money priv-ileged girls may spend on their hair before they enter middle school, even coloring their hair. Children's hair is thin and fragile; it gets stronger as they mature. Their scalps also are very sensitive and aller-gic reactions happen readily, so no permanent or semi-permanent hair color should be used at young ages. Temporary washout colors are safer but highlighting and hair lightening are dangerous until after puberty.[8] Considering the risks and the unknowns relative to the safety of hair dyes for children, saying "no" to unnecessary toxins is a true "yes" in my mind.

As with other aspects of body image, we simply do not age out of our hair concerns. Think of how the increased divorce rate puts so many women back in the dating scene at midlife. Whether one is single or separated, straight and cisgendered or LGBTQI, hair takes on a new meaning when one is "looking for love." Feeling attractive and current with the latest styles can be paramount concerns: hair is almost always a major factor in this equation. For women returning to the workplace after taking time out for their families, hair color is also a major concern—they want to be seen as young and vibrant, and hair, especially its color, is one way to convey that.

Women feel less at peace with their appearance as they age than they ever have. Each year these concerns seem to intensify. In today's half-changed world, increasing numbers of women are in the workplace, often in jobs previously off-limits, but unprecedented pressures surrounding appearance accompany these opportuni-ties. Whether a laborer, a contractor, an engineer, or a pilot, women sometimes feel the need to show their femininity to offset a mas-culine career choice. Hair may be the answer as many of these jobs exclude any creativity in clothing.

Hair is often a hot issue for those in the LGBTQI community. Some lesbian women feel they need to be super-girly to be accepted in the straight world. This is especially likely if they are not ready to come out yet, do not have family support, or are in a hostile or rejecting social or work environment. Others may want to convey a more masculine image. In any case, hair can deliver a powerful message.

For transgender women (male to female), the entire hair experience may be anxiety-producing. Just walking into a hair salon can be like landing on another planet. Hair salons are unique subcultures. Even as a cisgender heterosexual, I am not sure how comfortable I would feel in that environment if hair salons had not been part of my upbringing.

Since long hair is so intertwined with femininity, many transwomen want to grow their hair—not an easy transition, especially if they are older and already have had some hair loss. Wigs and hairpieces can help, but they introduce the transwoman to a whole new part of the beauty industry, not to mention the time and expense involved to find what works best for that individual. Remember—few transgender women have the money and resources that someone like Caitlyn Jenner has. The transgender community may be supportive and creative, but our culture is still very traditionally gendered and not easy to navigate for nontraditional souls.

Women of color have much to teach us about the multiple layers of the meaning of hair. Later chapters (Chapters 13–14) delve into this. Suffice it to say black and brown women often find themselves in a culture that seems to want to whitewash everything about them. Hair can be a major battlefield if their natural look is strikingly different than the standard Caucasian image.

For most women, their hair story will have many chapters before being put to rest. Even at funerals, mourners frequently comment about the dead woman's hairstyle, both how it looks on that day and what it meant to her throughout her life.

"Pay Attention to Your Hair..."

With a rich history, hair is a powerful language, and, like other aspects of body image, is a highly sensitive subject for most women.

In 2013, First Lady Michelle Obama's new look—the same hairstyle but with bangs—prompted intense scrutiny. Her hair and fashion choices sometimes seemed more important in the popular press than her husband's inauguration for his second term as the first African American president of the United States.

A negative hair comment is a quick and surefire way to hurt another woman. During a hotly contested Senate race in California a few election cycles back, Republican newcomer Carly Fiorina criticized the two-term Democrat incumbent Senator Barbara Boxer, saying, "God, what is that hair? Soooooooo yesterday."[9] Fiorina herself had very short, post-chemotherapy hair, making this criticism somewhat tone-deaf—an older version of the stereotypical mean girl.

With more and more women competing for higher office, for better or worse, hair may become part of both the campaign and the commentary. Having learned this the hard way, then-senator Hillary Rodham Clinton told a Yale College graduating class: "Your hair will send significant messages to those around you: what hopes and dreams you have for the world, but more, what hopes and dreams you have for your hair. Pay attention to your hair because everyone else will."[10]

Her words continue to ring true. Later, when serving as secretary of state, undoubtedly the most powerful position in the international diplomacy, Clinton grew her hair shoulder-length, and it soon became the focus of countless news stories. She had little time for hair care, and this style was the easiest and least time-consuming. Negotiating peace in the Mideast seems a bit more important than anyone's hair, secretary of state or not, but hair can always be a lightning rod for criticism. Joking about the media's obsession with her hair while on the 2016 spring presidential campaign trail, she offered: "You're not going to see me turning white in the White House."[11]

Meanwhile, men can be gray, balding, or bald, and it never affects public opinion in the same way. In fact, these signs of aging—or "maturity"—often give them more credibility and respect.

Clinton—the former first lady herself, as well as a prominent senator and secretary of state and later the first female nominee for president and the winner of the popular vote—was right: everyone will pay attention to a woman's hair, especially if she has power. Ironically, there is a silver lining to this sad truth, as she says in this positive reframe: "If I want to knock a story off the front page, I just change my hairstyle."[12]

We may be well into the 21st century, but all this history shapes what we see in the mirror each day and the meaning and power we ascribe to this one physical characteristic. Only when we understand what hair means within a greater political, social, and cultural system can our hair truly be our hair, rather than a relic of these other forces playing out in our lives. Hair is a unique component in the "body self" and in a woman's identity.

History:
The Roots of the Past

CHAPTER 3

It's Never Just Hair

"Like restless spirits that belong neither to this world nor the next, hair has been invested with a totemic power by ancients and moderns alike.... In the hands of a malefactor, one's hair became one's weak and unprotected self."—Diane Simon[1]

Despite its central role in women's lives across historical eras, cultures, and socio-economic strata, hair has been largely excluded from the research and conversations among the experts in psychology and psychiatry. The exception is Carl Jung (1875–1961), the Swiss psychiatrist who was the first to examine the deeper meanings of the ordinary experiences of everyday life, culminating in his groundbreaking work on consciousness, symbolism, and archetypes.[2] An early disciple of Sigmund Freud, he eventually rejected Freud's emphasis on sex as the primary motivator of human behavior. Instead, Jung believed that human experience is affected by far more than our conscious mind and memories can explain.[3]

Jung's broader framework conceptualized the psyche as a complicated integration of three different spheres: the conscious ego, the personal unconscious, and the collective unconscious. Hair reflects and incorporates all three spheres.

Meaning, Mana and Magic

Although hair is a visible symbol seen in media images everywhere in our social environment, the topic of hair is not as superficial as it may first appear. In his seminal work on consciousness, symbolism, and archetypes, Jung systematically examined the deeper

27

meanings of the ordinary experiences of everyday life. He emphasized symbols, underlying patterns, and truths, conceptualizing hair as the outer expression of the inner self, with hair imagery in dreams always reflecting a deeper meaning—magical, spiritual, or both.

In Jung's schema, messy hair means we are confused or mixed up; knotted hair represents uncertainty, maybe what we are *not* thinking about; uncombed hair means we need to straighten out; matted hair suggests unbalanced thoughts; hair falling out suggests a loss of power or being drained. In other words, decisions about combing, cutting, curling, or coloring hair reflect the integration of our outer and inner experiences: the conscious and the deeply unconscious. In fact, because so many of Jung's patients dreamed that he cut or *bobbed* their hair, he decided a *barber* was the best symbol of the analyst's role.[4] While at first that may seem an odd association, anyone who spends time in a hair salon overhears clients confiding in their stylist as if they were talking to a trusted therapist. The care of our hair and the care of our spirit go hand in hand for many women.

Sorcery and Healing

According to Jung, many primitive cultures believed that hair holds *mana*, a pervasive vital force capable of considerable influence on human life and magical healing. Legend has it that spirits—both good and bad—enter the body through the hair so witches and healers often used a lock of hair to work their magic. In ancient times, hair cut from the head or a beard was sacrificed as a favor to gods, and medicine men would attach hair to vessels holding their healing tonics or potions to protect or enhance their power. Jung describes that in earlier cultures, after a haircut, great care was taken to collect all strands or else a sorcerer or a witch could use them to cast a spell on people.[5] Native American tribes generally believed that others could use their hair against them so they would not allow their enemies any contact with their hair and would burn any stray hairs.[6]

Throughout history, many cultures have believed that hair

contains and reflects a person's life force or personal essence.[7] According to the Greek myth of Mnemosyne, her hair stored her exceptional memory, while in the Old Testament, Samson's strength was in his hair, not in his muscles. Sumo wrestlers also supposedly store their strength in their hair and cutting their hair announces the end of their careers.[8] Big hair is of utmost importance in New Guinea where tribesmen believe that the ghosts of ancestors are lodged in one's hair and baldness symbolizes abandonment by one's ancestors—not a good sign spiritually.[9]

In the Incan empire, and in some tribal cultures today, the antidote for poison often includes burnt ashes from a lock of the individual's hair. A commonly held belief in Imperial Rome (from 27 BCE to 476 CE) warned that washing your hair would disturb the spirit that guards the head, so it should be limited to once a year (specifically on August 13, the birthday of the goddess Diana).[10] Other cultures have recommended similar caution, respecting the unique power of hair. In contrast, today, we layer chemical after chemical on our hair—shampoos, conditioners, detanglers, mousses and gels, volumizers, straighteners, sprays, Keratin, masks, glosses, and the list goes on. We see our hair as needing more treatment and more chemical assistance, never as a spiritual storage space that should not be disturbed. As you will see in Chapter 6, much money is made this way, elevating hair to the status of a major player in the modern economy.

Regeneration, Renewal and Reflection

Its physical properties make hair a truly unique human characteristic. Perhaps because it grows throughout our lifespan, hair is often seen as a symbol of regeneration or renewal.[11] It feels no pain when we cut it, and it continues to grow—it survives, as if it were both dead and alive at the same time. In contrast to the rest of the body, hair continues to grow throughout our lives, decomposes very slowly, and when a body is sealed in a tomb after death, it lasts for thousands of years—much longer than any other human remain. Unlike any other body part, hair can exist independent of our bodies—it can be cut and made into a wig, hairpiece or talisman and still maintain its recognizable form.[12]

Since hair remains so stable over time, it is a great reminder; a lock of hair from a famous person or a loved one is a priceless treasure and a tangible and timeless memory. Mothers often keep some from their children's first haircuts, and mourners often cut a lock of hair from the corpse of loved ones to keep as a connection to them. This tradition appears to be timeless, dating back to ancient cultures, but it became more popular in the 1700s when people began to use lockets to hold these mementos of their romantic partners, loved ones, or children. In the Victorian era, mourning jewelry evolved as another way to honor the deceased. Hair of the dead loved one was placed in a glass brooch and later the hair of others could be added at their deaths.[13]

The hair of celebrities and historical figures also has attracted much interest, sometimes auctioned for charity fundraising. In his collection, John Reznikoff, a world-renowned expert in rare and historic documents and memorabilia, has hair from figures such as Abraham Lincoln, Beethoven, Napoleon and more modern celebrities like Michael Jackson, Elvis Presley, and Marilyn Monroe. He notes that in Victorian days, people asked celebrities for a piece of their hair the way we ask for autographs[14] or selfies today. Hair is never just hair—it provides a deep and comforting connection, crossing the barriers of time and even death.

In addition to conveying such rich personal, social, and cultural meanings, hair is actually a historical and living record, revealing accurate, factual information about us, even long after we die. Our organs are constantly breaking down and replacing themselves. For example, every five days, our stomach lining is replaced; every six weeks, our livers have a whole new lining; and each month, our skin sloughs off and duplicates itself.[15]

Hair is different. Our only feature to have a lifespan of four to seven years, it tells the history of what we have eaten, what drugs or other substances we have ingested, and other important information affecting our health.[16] Unlike our other organ systems, it continues to tell those stories for years. Physicians sometimes use hair analysis in the diagnostic process, determining deficiencies in important minerals or exposure to toxins such as heavy metals. Forensic experts also depend on hair analysis to answer many questions and, as pharmaceutical research advances, hair analysis may present an alternative to urinalysis. The DNA in our hair is in fact more reliable than fingerprints for personal identification.[17] And hair is easily available at crime scenes as both the perpetrator and the victim shed it routinely.[18] Hair always tells a story.

While we often think of it as an inert substance, hair is in fact an important sensory device for humans, an extension of our nervous system, expanding the sense of touch beyond our skin. It senses movement, like from wind, insects, or other elements. When we are shocked or scared, our "guard hairs" stand up, just as we notice on animals.[19] Hair also senses external temperature and adjusts to keep us warm. The tiny arrector pili muscles surrounding our hair filaments press upward, so the hair on our bodies and heads stands up and provides some protection and insulation. The technical term is piloerection, but we know it better as "goose bumps." In the heat, our hair lies flat instead, allowing our bodies to cool off. Hair is both intuitive, reacting to and interpreting external stimulation, and expressive of our internal states.

Our physical history is not the only record our hair keeps—our cultural and emotional histories are also woven into those strands. Coming of age rituals in many cultures include a dramatic change in hairstyle. For example, in Sierra Leone, at puberty, girls are brought to a special camp where their hair is cut as a rite of passage. Once their hair is long enough again, it is braided at a public ceremony, designating their new status as young adults. Some Indigenous tribes allow young women to grow their hair long only when they reach a certain age. The Hopi nation has a style called the squash blossom or the butterfly that designates the girl being ready for marriage. Coming of age rituals for males may also include hair being cut or even shaved to show his preparation for adult life and marriage.[20]

Recognizing that hair can symbolically hold grief, loss, fear, and pain, cutting hair after the death of a loved one is a routine part of the mourning process in many cultures. Brahmin women shave their heads when widowed and are supposed to remain this way, wearing white for the rest of their lives to pronounce their celibacy.[21] Today, women often use a dramatic change of their hairstyle, especially a haircut, to usher in a new life stage after a relationship ends, a divorce or other losses. That new hairdo is like a new lease on life and a means of leaving the past behind. In fact, a quick look at her hair in an old photo will instantly remind a woman of how she felt and what life issues she was facing when the photo was taken.

Jung was right—hair is full of mana and meaning and magic. It always tells a story, often reflecting our deepest and innermost individual feelings and social traditions.

I Am My Hair

Intergenerational conflicts often play out in differences in music and in hairstyles. Younger generations use their hair and their music loudly and proudly to separate themselves from the status quo. Baby Boomers like me readily remember how hair figured prominently as a metaphor of change in the 1960s, placing the messages of the hippie counterculture front and center in the first rock musical, *Hair*, asking for people to "flow it, show it. Long as God can grow it."[22] Today, countless songs about hair can be found, from the Christian rock song titled "Big Hair Gets You Closer to God"[23] to Lady Gaga's release of "Hair" on her album *Born This Way* in 2011, begging to be accepted and loved for who she is: "And I want you to know, I am my hair."[24] In my conversations with women, so many echo those exact words: "I am my hair."

Hair tells the story of women's lives like nothing else does. Playing a central role in the battles for power, self-determination, and autonomy, hair functions almost like a second, but nonverbal, universal language, as women struggle to assert their own authority and often to escape their status as second-class citizens. Hair represents power, especially for women.

CHAPTER 4

Hair Throughout History

"Hair does not have a fixed meaning. It's like a conduit for social codes."—Yves Le Fur, curator of "Cheveux Cheris"[1]

The use of hair as a symbol, or a code for unspoken but powerful dynamics, is not new. The care, appearance, and even color of hair has held meaning since the earliest evidence of human life, seen in statues dating back to the Ice Age (25,000–30,000 BCE) and artwork, mythology, and folklore ever since. A special exhibit at the Musee du quai Branly in Paris in 2013 chronicled how humans have cut, styled, and used their hair to express critical individual, social, and political sentiments since 21,000 BCE through the 21st century. From the indigenous art of Africa, Asia, Oceania, and the Americas, through antiquity to the present, hair has demonstrated a fluid and dynamic meaning across cultures and eras. I was fortunate to see this exhibit in person and was moved beyond words.

The first descriptions of a human depict a being whose hair grew mostly on the head, making it a distinctly human characteristic. In prehistoric times, humans had much more hair, like other mammals, but as we began to clothe ourselves and to use fire and shelter to stay warm, we no longer needed as much protection from the elements. What had resembled an animal's fur coat later evolved into a light layer on our bodies, but hair remained on the top of our heads to protect the cranium and the brain inside. Less body hair made it easier to stay clean, avoid parasites and other health threats, and increased the amount of skin, allowing sex organs to be more visible and enhancing sexual sensitivity.[2]

No longer as necessary to survival, hair gradually assumed a cultural meaning that has continued to evolve. While other animals, especially primates, engage in grooming, humans are the only ones to alter our hair and use it decoratively or symbolically to signal important individual, social, or political messages.

Hair and Soul: Ancient Africa

Ancient African cultures conceptualized the head as the center of control, identity, and even the means for communication with the divine. In fact, as it is the closest body part to the heavens, any communication from the gods or spirits of the beyond was believed to pass through the hair to reach the soul. In some rituals, hair was left to hang loose, allowing evil spirits to leave and good spirits to enter the head. Later, the barber would cut and then style the hair close to the head to keep good spirits close and reject the evil spirits. Hair was seen as a source of power that could be used for good or evil.[3]

Artifacts from ancient Africa depict hair and its grooming as important traditions and rituals, elevating hairdressers to a high social status for their contributions. With the individual's spirit thought to be nestled in their hair, its care and grooming has always been a central part of African life. The "hairdresser" was deeply respected and generally seen as the most trustworthy member of the community.[4] Many of the ancient rituals and beliefs related to hair live on in traditional African societies, with some of today's intricate hairstyles in Nigeria dating back more than 2,000 years.

Each Nigerian tribal group has a unique ceremonial hairstyle, to which the royal family owns exclusive rights. Hair artists pass down their craft to their daughters in a time honored and respected lineage. In his photo collections of Nigerian hairstyles, 'Okhai Ojeikere, a photographer dedicated to promoting appreciation of his Nigerian culture, archives this remarkable cultural treasure, demonstrating hair as its own art form.[5]

Despite these rich, long-standing traditions honoring hair, once the slave trade emerged, masters often shaved the heads of African enslaved people, taking away both their cultural identity and their individual dignity. An enslaved person's living conditions did not allow for much attention to hair, so men often kept their heads shaved and women covered their scalps with rags.[6] Separating African Americans from their historical connection with their hair was a dehumanizing act and illustrates the critical importance of hair to the individual as well as to the social and political structures. Hair is easily used to control, demean, and disempower people, evident in this treatment and in the ongoing distinctions between "good hair" and the natural hair of most African Americans in more recent history. (See Chapters 13 and 14.)

"For all of it obviousness, its ordinariness, and its universality,
hair is still mysterious, possessing an uncanny ability
to shock, surprise, offend, and confound."
—SCOTT LOWE[7]

Hair and Hierarchy: Egypt

As long as 5,000 years ago, hair was a central part of life in ancient Egypt, with artwork showing mourners tearing out their hair when wailing at funerals and archaeologists finding recipes for anti-baldness remedies, hair dyes, and conditioners. The Egyptians even included a "barber god," Tua-ur, in their deities.[8] In fact, hair assumed such importance that barbers were also medicine men and priests, performing religious ceremonies, dentistry, and surgery, and serving as powerful figures in their communities. The red and white spiraling stripes of the old-fashioned, but still familiar, barber pole symbolized the integration of the two crafts of surgery and barbering, as hair care and body care were considered inseparable.[9] These two professions remained joined together until the 1700s, when medical discoveries were taking off rapidly, requiring more specific training to assure the best patient care.[10]

During the Egyptian era, complicated hairdos were the norm for both sexes, using a fire-heated version of a curling iron or materials like mud, clay, or beeswax to keep it in place. The use of dyes to cover gray hair but also to create bright colors—copper from henna

35

and bright blue from indigo—was common, as were wigs, despite the heat of the sun in that climate. Wigs, initially made from animal hair or from plant fibers such as cotton or palm leaf, and later (after 1550 BCE) made from human hair, were a status symbol, often buried with the dead body to maintain this prominence while entering the next world. Cleopatra, the queen of Egypt and later of the Roman Empire, had countless wigs.[11] While Egyptian pharaohs and the members of their royal families had their slaves carefully pluck their scalps completely to prepare for the wig, the law dictated that these servants had no choice but to wear their own hair.[12] Using hair to express issues such as social rank, attractiveness, or value is a long and deeply rooted tradition.

Artifacts and inscriptions illustrate that for women of the higher classes, hair care rituals among the aristocrats were often a social time, with enslaved servants providing the styling, children and friends visiting, and musicians playing, in scenes depicted as quite sensual and indulgent. Scents were pressed into the fatty oils and pomade used to fashion the hair, creating a multi-sensory impact. Even then, the style and the degree of grooming devoted to hair communicated critical messages about gender, age, and social rank.[13] Hair can quickly and easily delineate the "haves" from the "have-nots" in any era or society.

Sexuality and Status: Greek and Roman Traditions

In ancient Greece, hair was also an important and highly valued personal commodity. Hippocrates, seen as the father of modern medicine, made potions with opium, wine, oils, horseradish, and other ingredients for baldness, while a woman's hair immediately announced her social status: either a crown of privilege and virtue or a sign of servitude or shame. During this era, women began lightening their hair using rinses and rubbing it with pomades of pollen and yellow flower petals. Lighter hair soon represented enhanced social status and sexual attractiveness. Hair also reflected issues of sexuality and trust, with women in the Doric period (4th–5th centuries BCE) cutting their hair on their wedding day to renunciate vanity and show humility. Regarding women as men's property, jealous husbands would sometimes shave their wives' heads to control them and make them less attractive.[14]

Hair featured prominently with the rise of Roman culture (ca. 27 BCE–476 CE) as appearance and grooming were thought to reveal one's character as well as social status and religion. During this time, after many failed remedies for his gradual hair loss, Julius Caesar created the original comb-over, and Empress Faustina owned more than 700 wigs in every color and length available, enjoying the quick change in appearance and persona each hairpiece could evoke.[15] Ovid, the prolific Roman author of *Metamorphoses*, the epic tome of Greco-Roman mythology, and a major influence on later writers such as Shakespeare, Chaucer, Dante and Milton, even incorporated hair into his poetry.[16] Very early in the 1st century CE, Ovid wrote a poem that translates into modern language as "And I can't be comprehensive about hair-fashions when every day brings out a chic new style."[17] Later in another poem, again translated into modern vernacular, he chastised a lover for a bad hair decision, advising that it would grow back in time. Hair was a serious subject for lovers then, just as it is now.

During this era, a Roman woman of high society had as many as 200 enslaved servants taking care of her, each with a different job. The expectations for all these servants were high but were most extreme with the ornatrix who was trained to do her hair. Pity the poor servant if a curl was imperfect or out of place—hair was critically important in the social hierarchy, and dissatisfied aristocrats would even beat their maids when disappointed with their hair.[18]

These historical accounts demonstrate how routinely hair has been tied to class and social hierarchy. Hair can instantly announce one's social rank but, too often, the attendants who help to achieve that status are poorly treated and unrecognized for their talents and hard work. Hair, hierarchy, status, and power are always intertwined, and, once more, hair is never just hair.

Universal and Timeless

Hair has consistently been seen as a link to the power and energy of its original source. Symbolizing deep strength, strands of hair and full scalps have historically been used in trophies, totems, and rituals to carry energy, with the intent to bring future fertility and prosperity, to assure peace with deceased relatives, or to assure victory over enemies and evil forces. In Indonesian, Polynesian, and other cultures, hair has long been part of their weaponry, while in Native American tribes, scalping assumed various meanings from revenge to prestige to the acquisition of the power and spirit of the scalped party.[19]

Hair not only maintains a connection with the past, but it also serves as a link to the future. Yao women in China traditionally only have their hair cut once—when they turn 16. It is then woven into a symbolic headdress and given to the groom at their marriage, linking the bride to her family while she moves into the next stage in her life. Next it becomes part of her everyday hairdo, integrated with her growing hair and with stray or fallen hairs that are collected and added each day. A woman's hair is seen as a great asset and long hair is associated with wealth, longevity, and good luck.[20]

Hair serves to connect the generations and the living with the dead. In New Caledonia, the Kanak "mourning priests" grow theirs for three years, then cut it to create giant domes of hair mounted upon wood and feather masks for mourning rituals, connecting the mourners to their deceased ancestor and giving them the strength to move forward in life.[21]

Hair Today, Gone Tomorrow

Sacrificing one's hair serves a central role in the induction to many religious orders, signifying the renunciation of the body and sexuality as well as the willingness to give up something that has been important to them. To this day, Buddhist monks still shave their heads while modern charities, especially those seeking a cure for cancer, frequently sponsor events like a "shave for the cure," intending that this shared gesture of sacrificing human hair will usher in hope and remedies for the sufferers. A movement in the United States to support children with cancer started with the expression "bald kids rock," acknowledging the impact of chemotherapy, and evolved into Bald Moms Rock, when 46 mothers of children with cancer sponsored a "brave the shave" event, joining them in baldness to raise awareness and funding of pediatric cancer.[22] These mothers report a sense of empowerment and a deeper connection with their children when they "shave for the brave." While honoring and celebrating their children, they have simultaneously raised millions of dollars.

Throughout biblical and literary references, folklore, and contemporary pop culture, hair figures prominently and repeatedly. Considered the oldest religion in the world, Hinduism encourages followers to cut or sacrifice their hair, symbolizing a willingness to let go of their egos and worldly concerns and to devote themselves to God. Hindu families shave their children's heads to rid them of any impurities and allow fresh and new hair to grow and promote strength, energy, and other virtues including a long life. The sacrifice of hair remains a Hindu tradition today, as people travel to temples asking the gods for favors such as prosperous crops. The hair is then collected and sent for processing to be made into wigs and hairpieces, generating funds for many important services in India.[23] Spirituality and sacrifice, vanity and profit-making all coexist in the world of hair.

From ancient times onward, hair, devotion, and power have been closely tied, for both men and women. In the story of Samson and Delilah from the Old Testament, Samson is powerful until Delilah tricks him and his hair is cut: with it goes any power he held. Descriptions of the Last Supper include Mary Magdalen's act of devotion, washing and drying Christ's feet with her hair. During the 5th century, the "Frankish kings" who ruled France were known as the hair kings. Their long hair and beards symbolized their power, and any challengers paid the price of having their heads shaved. A shaved head was such a disgrace that some of the upstarts chose death instead as a punishment.[24]

39

Traditional folklore portrays hair as a woman's greatest treasure. Feminist writer Susan Brownmiller reminds us that every fairy princess has long hair and that short hair has generally represented a loss of femininity.[25] Fairy tales usually depict a pretty girl like Rapunzel, who uses her long hair to be rescued from her life imprisoned and alone in a tower. Today's Disney princesses tend to have long hair as well, from Cinderella, Tinkerbell, and Snow White to Jasmine, Belle and Ariel, with YouTube tutorials advising how to create the style and many products available to purchase and assure the perfect rendition. Speaking of the commercial value of hair, the best-selling Barbie doll of all time was the 1992 edition of Totally Hair Barbie, with tresses spanning from her head to her toes—10 million were sold, making her a record setter.[26]

In keeping with the folklore traditions, literature has also characterized hair as an invaluable asset for women. In the classic novel *Little Women*,[27] Jo sells her hair to help her family survive. In the familiar Christmas story *The Gift of the Magi*,[28] a poor couple sacrifices their greatest treasures to buy each other a gift, with hers being her beautiful brown hair. In the short story "Bernice Bobs Her Hair," F. Scott Fitzgerald, the iconic, hip, and fast-living writer of the "Roaring 20s," wrote an early version of today's mean girls, played out through devastating hair advice.[29] The plot concerns the rivalry between two young cousins, with shy and awkward Bernice seeking social approval and her jealous, queen bee cousin Marjorie recommending a daringly modern hair cut for Bernice—the bob. The new 'do was a disaster, ending any social capital Bernice had earned. Before leaving town in the middle of the night, Bernice vengefully cuts her cousin's hair as she sleeps, so both suffer from bad hair.

Hair has been and continues to be a metaphor and a medium for deeper cultural, social, and political issues. While it can both attract and unify, it also can repel and separate. We need to understand and respect this complexity. Never just hair, it is often about power and domination.

CHAPTER 5

Hair, Sexuality and Gender Politics

"Any choice a woman makes carries extra meaning: it leads observers to conclude something about the type of person she is."—Deborah Tannen[1]

Hair figures prominently in the gender politics of an era. Even as the lines between genders blur and people are freer to express their innermost identity, many traditional binary images and perceptions persist.

For men, hair is generally a neutral feature. Look around a crowd at a ballgame, a lecture, a museum, a city street, or a shopping mall; most men have hair cut relatively short in no particular style. Unless we see a shaved head or a ponytail, we rarely think twice about it. But look at women in those same crowds and we find ourselves taking a much more detailed inventory of their hair.

In linguistic theory, hair "marks" women. No matter what the style, it always affects our assessments of women. She may be too focused on appearance or not focused enough. She may look beautiful, or she may look unhealthy, or a messy head may lead us to conclude that she is an unfit mother—we always have a reaction to a woman's hair.

One quick glance tells us if she is "butch" or "femme" and leads us to many more assumptions. Because women have more hair than men and experience much more pressure around appearance and fashion, hair occupies more space in their lives and in our impressions and beliefs. As linguist Deborah Tannen writes, "there is no unmarked woman."[2]

Gender Politics: Alive and Well

Even in the 21st century, with all the progress women have made, our attitudes toward women's hair and other aspects of appearance remind us that we still have far to go to reach gender equity. According to Deborah Rhode, one of the most accomplished women in the U.S. legal system and author of *The Beauty Bias: The Injustice of Appearance in Life and Law*,[3] "the issues women face relative to appearance and body image are the issues we have made the least progress in changing."[4] These are not cosmetic issues—our ongoing focus on appearance only perpetuates the gender hierarchies, keeping women in their place as trophy wives or sex objects rather than as equal partners in relationships and the workplace. Ironically, as feminism has opened so much of the world to women, our comfort with our natural hair has shrunk.

Dr. Rhode had her own story to tell about the role hair still plays in the power structure. Despite her endless accomplishments—as the director of the Center on the Legal Profession at Stanford University and formerly president of the Association of American Law Schools, chair of the American Bar Association's Commission on Women in the Profession, and director of Stanford's Institute for Research on Women—her hair was a lightning rod for criticism. As she climbed the ladder of achievement, obviously gifted intellectually and capable beyond description, and her exposure within the university and then within the national associations grew, so did the scrutiny of her appearance.

When she was scheduled to speak as chair of the American Bar Association's Commission on Women in the Profession, a media consultant for the ABA let Dr. Rhode know that "the tension was mounting" over how she would look on screen, offering to pay for a personal shopper and a makeup and hair stylist. PR staff surveyed her wardrobe and found one outfit that was minimally acceptable to them, but very early on the day of the luncheon, two stylists arrived at her hotel room, teasing, spraying, and styling up a storm. Although the layers of makeup survived the humidity when she left the hotel, her hair drooped instantly, causing criticism and dismay to the PR staff and other stakeholders. Ironically, the organization she represented is dedicated to women's advancement in the legal profession and in the world. The association insisted on the same ritual for the next year's event, despite what seemed to be not only the ultimate mixed message about women and achievement but also a waste of the association's dollars.

Professor Rhode laughed about this and the similar scenarios she has faced when her competence is discarded but her look is magnified. Confident and comfortable in her skin and in her intellect, she knows exactly who she is, so this amused her. As she said to me: "I am reasonably convinced that every day of my life I've had a bad hair day—my junior prom, my wedding day, and when being inaugurated as president of the Association of American Law Schools." For women less certain of themselves and their value as human beings, however, such messages can be devastating.

Consistently, women are held hostage to concerns about their appearance in ways that men never are, and hair is a major player in this scenario. Gender expectations were alive and well when the country was up in arms learning that 2008 presidential candidate John Edwards spent $400 on a haircut. In contrast, no one commented on the $40,000 the Republican National Committee paid for Sarah Palin's hair stylist to travel with her (approximately $750 per day) during her campaign as the vice presidential nominee that same year or the $68,000 spent on her makeup artist.[5] Professor Rhode is quick to point out that, compared to other gender inequities, like violence, reproductive justice, and equal employment and pay, hair may be a minor issue but it still disempowers women day in and day out. We need to be more aware of how this plays out in our lives both individually and culturally.

Customs and beliefs about hair often reveal an underlying distrust of women, fear of their sexuality, and attempts at controlling them by controlling their hair. As with foot-binding and other cultural traditions, a woman trying to meet the current beauty standards, intending to elevate her status and image, is simultaneously disempowered. Consider the 17th and 18th centuries, when the dominant fashions for hair included complicated wireframes and gadgets, piling long hair on top of a woman's head. This made holding her head up exhausting, getting in and out of carriages tricky, and neck pain and headaches normal. Many had to sleep sitting up to keep their hair intact. At least one British noblewoman died after her tall, highly-styled hair caught on fire, and near-fatal accidents were commonplace.[6] Some might call this pure fashion, but others see it as an attempt to disempower women by controlling their hair and a potential object of passion and sexual energy.

Never Neutral

Scroll forward to the 21st century. Once more, for women working their way up the corporate ladder, hair is not a neutral issue. Gender and power issues are always in the mix. When she was being considered for a promotion to the upper executive inner circle of a high-tech company a few years ago, Mary Lou was told she had to cut her hair—no questions asked. She had luscious, thick, wavy, henna-colored hair. While this felt like a huge assault, she also did not believe she had much choice in this matter. If she wanted to advance in the corporate world, she would have to pay this price. She never let her hair grow back until retirement—she experienced this as a non-negotiable demand in her career advancement.

Women working in the media, especially news broadcasting, are told exactly the length, style, and color to wear, and they may have their hair "done" two, three or more times a day, depending on the number of broadcasts or appearances. That is a lot of handling and exposure to chemical products. Although not written into the job description, perfect hair can be a requirement for hiring, retention, and promotion. Diane Smith, a television anchorwoman and Emmy-winning producer, journalist, and best-selling author, described her experience:

> You are talking to a woman who was told how long her hair could be, how it should be styled, and what color it could be.
> A woman who could turn in a top news story, while reporting in difficult weather conditions, and get called on the carpet for flyaway hair.
> A woman who had her hair done twice a day, 5 days a week, for 10 years![7]

For African American women or others with natural curls and kinks, hair and the visual media workplace may be enemy environments, as the stylists often have had no experience with their hair texture or style, sometimes leading to disaster. (See Chapters 13 and 14.) Needless to say, men are rarely subject to such scrutiny or standards.

Despite their physical feats, even the most accomplished female athletes routinely face criticism for their hair. The 2021 Olympics (postponed from 2020 due to the global pandemic) set its own personal best for inclusion of women—49 percent of the athletes were female.[8] That aspect of the playing field was nearly equal—an exciting moment for the whole world. Yet, other aspects of the playing field are far from equal. An San, a 20-year-old South Korean, won three gold medals in women's archery and beat a record in the qualifying rounds that had been in place for 25 years. Despite these victories, she became the target of scathing sexist criticism for her short haircut, accusing her of "being a feminist," as if that is a bad thing.

Responding on Instagram to why she cut her hair, An San stated simply, "Because it's comfortable." A social media movement erupted (#women_shortcut_campaign) with scores of women uploading pictures of their own short haircuts.[9] With everything else going on during the 2021 Olympics, this attack on a woman athlete who was literally at the top of her sport was a mind-boggling reminder of how much more work we have to do to level the playing field and accept the decisions women make about their bodies—and their hair—as theirs alone.

Gender, power, and hair are a package deal—quite a trifecta.

Sexuality

Hair has long been associated with female sexuality, engendering both attraction and distrust. Myths and folklore about women sirens and mermaids, who seduced sailors by singing while they combed their long hair, have traditionally depicted women's hair as a dangerous and seductive force. According to the story of Lorelei,[10] this beautiful blond, heartsick after a lover never returned, would sit

45

on rocks on the Rhine River waiting for him, singing softly and luring sailors who would then be shipwrecked. Some versions of this story have Lorelei throwing herself into the water in despair, with her spirit continuing to distract sailors into danger. Earlier Greek myths portrayed the sirens as large birds with female heads who shed their avian qualities and become dangerous temptresses. Whether the ancient myth or the 19th-century version of Lorelei, the consistent message is that women, apt to use their beauty, especially their long tresses, to entrap and seduce men, should never be trusted.

Shaped by this view of female power and by the belief that women were more tempted by the devil and could thereby endanger men, early Christian leaders pressured women to cover their hair. By the 2nd century CE, they declared that women must always cover their heads in church.[11] Saint Paul's first letter to the Corinthians in the New Testament included the directive that men should have short hair and women should have long, but covered, hair as a sign of their faith in God: "Does not even nature itself teach you that if a man has long hair, it is a dishonor to him, but if a woman has long hair, it is a glory to her? For her hair is given to her for a covering" (1 Corinthians 11:14–15).[12]

Her "glory" of long hair was not meant as a compliment, but rather as an indicator that woman is less than man who, made in the image and likeness of God, is free to worship with an uncovered head.[13] Somehow a woman's hair came to be seen as both sacred and profane, covering her body but also conveying her sexuality, setting her up for shame, self-doubt, and disempowerment. Although hair was to be covered, controlled long hair, especially blond hair, was cherished. At one point, the Catholic church did not allow women to cut their hair and could excommunicate them for this.[14] The correlations among purity, faith, the length of a woman's hair, and the directive that it be covered continue to be constants across many religious traditions.

The Wedding Veil

In Greek, Roman, and Jewish marriage customs, covering and uncovering the bride's hair figures prominently. In fact, the Latin word "nubere" translates as "to marry" but literally means to veil oneself. In most marriage rituals, the man's hair stays the same while the woman's changes,[15] perhaps representing the impact marriage will have on her life. After marriage, orthodox Jewish women are expected to cover their hair or to wear a wig, with this covering representing ownership: the woman now belongs to the man. In traditional Jewish law, a husband can divorce his wife simply by uncovering her hair. Or, if a wife uncovers her hair in public, she signifies infidelity, permitting the husband to divorce her and not return her dowry or provide financial support like alimony.[16] Some still follow these practices.

As a symbol, hair is literally just the surface of the transformation that marriage introduces to a woman's life. Earlier in the history of the United States, some states and local entities passed laws requiring a woman to get her husband's permission before cutting her hair.[17] The underlying premise was that the man owned his wife. Once more, hair is all about power. I assume that these laws have been overturned by now, but I worry that some may remain on the books.

To this day, traditional marriage customs typically include the bride being veiled, originally intended to control the tempting lure of her hair, then unveiled during the ceremony for all to witness. Often brides wear their hair up, then later let it down, as a flirtatious or sexual symbol. In some cultures, women cut their hair on their wedding day to demonstrate purity and humility, and jealous husbands shave their wives' heads.[18] Christian nuns, considered to be the "brides of Christ," historically have their hair short and covered by a white coif of thick and stiff material, part of their "habit," a set of garments specific to each religious order, to keep their hair as private as possible. Only in the past 50 years have nuns been allowed to unveil their heads and reveal their hair. Some religious communities have kept the habit or a short veil, but many modern orders now leave decisions about hair to the individual sister.

Veiling and covering hair with headscarves or wigs continue in many cultures. Religions like Islam and orthodox Judaism still insist on women's hair being covered whenever they are in public to demonstrate chastity or self-control and to avoid tempting men. Anthropologist Carol Delaney warns that these customs can only be understood in their culturally-specific frameworks.[19] For example, many Westerners see the veiling of women in Middle Eastern countries as outdated and oppressive to women, but Delaney's research indicates that its meaning varies widely among countries and subcultures. While in some instances women veil themselves due to religious devotion to Islam, others may do so as a sign of resistance to the influence of Western culture, and still others may be attempting to free themselves from the objectification of the male gaze. For some, the decision may be due to a blend of these sentiments.

Hair and Power

Taking away control over her hair is guaranteed to diminish a woman's spirit, to dehumanize and to punish her, and it has been used throughout history for just that purpose. During the French Revolution, a noblewoman's hair would be cut short before she was brought to the guillotine. While this may have made the act of beheading easier, it was also meant to shame and dehumanize the woman. Although Joan of Arc had already worn her hair very short, perhaps being the inspiration for the bob, her executioners shaved her head before her beheading, nonetheless. They also made her wear a dress, after she had worn armor and male garb for years, to protect herself from being raped while serving in the French military and then as a prisoner.[20]

It has not been unusual to shave the heads of prisoners or psychiatric patients to show their deviance. Before her royal beheading in 1536, the second wife of King Henry VIII, Anne Boleyn, had her head shaved. Marie Antoinette's was shaved when she was guillotined in the French Revolution in 1793. During World War II, the French shaved the heads of women who were friendly with German soldiers. The Nazis typically shaved the heads of Jews either before or after putting them to death to further annihilate their spirits and then sold the hair for profit.[21]

As the U.S. government gained control over Native American people by taking their land and ability to survive, they were forced to live on reservations and to give up many of their traditions. In 1865, a law was passed taking Native American children from their families and placing them in government-run boarding schools. In the process, their clothing and hairstyles, those important symbols of their heritage and roots, were no longer allowed. To Native Americans, short hair generally means that a woman is in a state of mourning for a loss or in a state of shame for a wrongdoing, while long hair is a connection to their spirituality. For a Native American girl, losing her tribal hairstyle and having her hair cut short is potentially traumatizing and confusing. Later, in the 20th century, these policies were reversed and indigenous people could once more maintain their own traditions,[22] yet their disempowerment has had a lasting marginalizing impact on their lives.

Making a Long Story Short

As women have assumed more rights and power in the 20th and 21st centuries, hairstyles have changed as well. In the United States during World War I, women worked in factories to support the war effort and began to cut their hair for safety and ease. After the war, adopting a short haircut known as "the bob" freed women from the time and effort involved with long hair. Within one short week in 1924, a New York salon bobbed the hair of 3,500 women—with some fainting and needing smelling salts in the process. By 1925, more than half of the students at Mount Holyoke, a well-known and well-respected women's college in the Northeast, had their hair bobbed, while other colleges unsuccessfully tried to ban these radical haircuts as well as other new trends like makeup and cigarettes.[23] Some women used the bob as a sign of emancipation and viewed the freedom from endless hair care rituals to be as liberating as the right to vote. They felt freer to dance, play sports, ride bicycles, and ride in convertibles—some daring women might even drive their own!

"I consider getting rid of our long hair one of the many little shackles that women have cast aside in their passage to freedom."
MARY GARDEN, OPERA DIVA, 1927[24]

Short hair may have been a sign of emancipation, but with this major change in women's roles and the balance of power between men and women came a backlash. Somehow, bobbed hair was going to make women "act like men," or make them wear short skirts and more makeup, or make them smoke, drink, and go out alone without a date accompanying her. She might even work in a less traditional job or have sex!

Charles Nessler, who invented the permanent wave machine, predicted that these short haircuts would weaken the scalp and cause women to go bald, just like men.[25] Preachers sermonized about the risky behaviors a bob might lead to, while some schools banned it or offered bonuses to teachers who kept their hair long.[26] Some businesses refused to hire women and even fired those who cut their hair. The iconic Chicago department store Marshall Field's publicly terminated the employment of a woman on the grounds that her short hair was "not dignified." Other Marshall Field's employees who bobbed their hair were required to wear hairnets till the hair grew. These actions garnered national attention with *The Nation* and the *New York Times* both raising this issue as a violation of personal liberty.[27] Around this same time, a nursing school in Kentucky suspended five students who cut their hair, buoyed by research at the University of Arkansas that "long haired women have the best minds."[28]

Monsieur Antoine, a Parisian later living in the United States, the creator of modern hairdressing and the first celebrity hairstylist, had developed a bob inspired by Joan of Arc's image and later introduced the shingle, cut shorter than the bob, exposing the ears, an even more radical style. In *Antoine by Antoine*,[29] he described these backlash events. Changing the norm for women's hair symbolized changing their role in American culture and that was not easy.

In the 1960s and 1970s, a period of significant social change, hair again played a key role in challenging power, race, and gender norms and traditions. With "hippies"—both men and women—wearing long, free-flowing, untamed hair, and more African Americans wearing it natural, states tried to use the law to control these forces by regulating hair. So many cases made it through the court system that U.S. Supreme Court Justice William O. Douglas commented: "Nothing is more indicative of the importance currently being attached to hair growth by the general populace than the barrage of cases reaching the courts evidencing the attempt by one segment of society to control the plumage of another."[30]

Countless cases alleging discrimination related to appearance and sex-based and race-based grooming practices continue to move through the courts. (See Chapter 14.) In today's workplace, women must maintain a professional image that traditionally has been based on white male standards. Hair is a central aspect to a woman's body image as well as a means of self-expression, making it an easy target. Women have filed suits alleging they were fired for not dying their hair to cover the gray (age discrimination), for not styling their hair (gender discrimination) or for wearing hair in natural dreadlocks (race discrimination).

In 2006, the ACLU filed a racial discrimination case against a Virginia Beach nightclub for prohibiting entry to anyone wearing braids, twists, cornrows, or dreadlocks, arguing that it targets hairstyles predominately worn by African Americans. Caucasian women with dramatically spiked hair dyed platinum and black were allowed admission while African American women wearing dreadlocks or cornrows were denied entry. The Department of Justice also filed a complaint alleging racial discrimination, reaching a settlement with the club, enforcing a non-discriminatory dress code policy and a system for receiving and investigating complaints of discrimination and monitoring to ensure non-discriminatory treatment of their patrons in a manner consistent with federal law.[31] (More on this issue in Chapter 14.)

Hair can be a powerful statement, challenging social and cultural rules and traditions and asserting one's individuality. Long hair, short hair, covered or uncovered, natural or highly styled—each expresses underlying statements about power, gender, and sexuality. The language of hair speaks sometimes through a whisper and other times with a roar.

CHAPTER 6

Hair Economics

"Genius is of small use to a woman who does not know how to do her hair."—Edith Wharton[1]

Hair, one of the most prominent human features, has assumed a leading role in women's personal narratives and self-images today. Consequently, women spend far more on their hair than men do, with the hope that this investment will "pay off" by advancing their career or increasing their earnings or by attracting attention and relationships to enhance their social status.

Today's media-driven era, saturated with unreasonable, constantly changing beauty ideals and standards, has turned the body into a form of currency for women, making their appearance as valuable as gold. Despite all the progress in the last century providing women opportunities for education, employment, athletics, and public service, women still earn far less than men in the United States. The estimate that female full-time workers on average earn 80 percent of what men earn for comparable jobs in the United States has become an urban legend. Sadly, it's not true. The reality is that white women earn 79 percent of what their male peers earn but African American and Hispanic women are paid far less—63 and 55 percent, respectively. Native American women earn 60 percent and Pacific Islanders 63 percent. Asian American women fare better at 87 percent, but still fall short of our white male peers. At the current rate of progress, women will not reach pay parity until the next century.[2]

These numbers are from 2019, prior to the pandemic so they do not reflect what has happened to women's economic health during this unprecedented time. Women have been human shock absorbers in this modern economic crisis. The global pandemic has hit them much harder than men, with many having to leave their jobs to take care of their children and participate in their homeschooling or virtual education. Employment outside of the home is just not possible for many women in these circumstances and their future employment and earnings are completely unknown, so these numbers may in fact be even more grim.

These gender-biased economic realities collude with unrelenting media images that associate "attractive" women's bodies with power. In addition to the gender gap in earnings, a "beauty premium" also exists. Attractive people may earn up to 12 percent more than less attractive peers—and this holds for both men and women. In fact, results of the 2018 Congressional midterm election were consistent with this finding, as the more attractive candidates were more likely to be elected.[3] Further fueled by a consumer culture and the incessant pressures to purchase the latest product and cosmetic advancement, this creates a perfect storm of female preoccupation with the body. This only complicates a woman's feelings about her hair, often making it a source of angst and worry and causing her to spend small fortunes of psychic energy, time, and money—all with the goal of being seen as acceptable, valuable, and wanted in our culture.

> *"Over the course of a lifetime, the average human spends more time messing with her or his hair ... than in nearly any other leisure activity. And we can't do it all by ourselves; most of us need help. Forget prostitution—I'm pretty sure hairstyling is the world's oldest profession."*
> —SCOTT LOWE[4]

Small Fortunes

In the consumer culture of the 21st century, hair plays as prominent a role in our economy as it does in our psychology. It may be impossible to calculate what U.S. women expend for hair care and hair products as money is spent in a variety of venues including homes or commercial salons, stores, and online. One survey of 2000 women estimates that the average U.S. woman will spend $55,000 on her hair in her lifetime. Women from California, Florida, or Texas will spend more, as the estimates of monthly spending vary state to state and those were at the high end, averaging $120 per month in contrast to $80.[5] The writer and filmmaker Nora Ephron struggled with her hair and other aspects of body image and appearance despite her overwhelming career success (*Sleepless in Seattle, When Harry Met Sally, Julie & Julia*). She visited her hair salon twice a week, confessing to being "completely inept at blow-drying my own hair." This translated into 80 hours per year at the salon—two full work weeks.[6] Ephron knows she could have been doing other things with all that time, but, once more, hair matters.

Hair is truly priceless, as we can never account for the hours or the price to the psyche and self-esteem of women who are constantly obsessing about what is happening on top of their heads.

A Global Issue

This investment of emotions, identity, and money is not limited to women in the United States; it is truly global. According to a report on global spending trends in the arena of personal care, hair care demonstrated the greatest increase. The total spending in the global beauty industry was $483 billion in 2020, with the expectation it will exceed $716 billion by 2025. The highest percentage—nearly a quarter—of that is spent on hair care. In the past, most of this was spent in retail stores, but since the pandemic, online sales now dominate, accounting for nearly half of the spending.[7]

Some projections suggest that the global hair care market was worth $86 billion in 2021. Market research estimates expect that by 2028 the global hair care market will exceed $134 billion,[8] while other estimates are even more extravagant. Regardless, hair is big business, with fortunes to be made—at least by big companies. How much trickles down to the actual stylist or salon is a very different story, unfortunately.

The reasons for this potential for economic growth are many.

With age comes dryness, thinning, decreased volume and gradual graying, creating a market for products that increase the fullness, shine, and color of youth. Pollution may have some of the same stressful effects on our hair, prompting us to spend more.

Rural populations are shrinking, metropolitan areas are growing, and, with the impact of global media and advertising, the fashion and beauty industries are infiltrating new territories. Shampoo is the largest product segment as more people now use it daily to counter pollution effects and are seeking new organic or natural products. Hair color is likely to be the fastest growing product in the 2020s, with fashion and appearance becoming more dominant across the globe. The pandemic may impact that income trajectory as more women are reverting to their natural hair color, but hair and hair color are economic drivers today.

National and international companies are systematically introducing new products and salons in rapidly developing cities and countries. Mergers, acquisitions, collaborations, and new product development are moving forward expeditiously. The United States has been the dominant force but India's contribution to this economic sphere is growing, especially in the niche of hair oil products, incorporated or used alone, particularly for aging, drying hair and hair affected by pollution factors. Market research also sees men as a growing market base and companies are gearing more products toward them.

While the United States, Europe and Japan are major markets, emerging markets like China, Brazil and India and developing nations will be instrumental in the economic growth of hair. In Japan, hair is already recognized as a barometer of the economy— women tend to wear it long during prosperous times but to cut it when the economy begins to slump.[9] Hair is a central ingredient of many economies across the globe.

---

*"When it comes to hair, I'm in the same boat as most
every other woman. The way we feel about our hair is universal—
we love it when it looks great, we can't stand it when it looks
not so great, and we all want it to tell the world something about us."*
—OPRAH[10]

The Good, The Bad, and the Ugly

Public or private, individual or cultural, here or there, hair always tells a story, but that story isn't always pretty.

Decades ago, feminist author Susan Brownmiller described how impoverished women had historically been pressured to sell their hair just as wet nurses sell their milk to support their families.[11] Hair is not only a global women's issue, but it is also closely tied to women's global economic well-being. Today, the demand for hair for wigs, weaves, and extensions is close to insatiable. In fact, according to Kim Kimble, a prominent Los Angeles hairstylist who designed a wig weighing three and a half pounds for Oprah to model on the cover of the special issue of *Oprah Magazine*, 90 percent of the women on the red carpet of events like the Oscars are wearing weaves, hair extensions, or clip-ins.[12] Few are there just with their own hair. This is truly "big business." Most of this hair comes from Asia, and most of the women selling this precious commodity will remain impoverished despite their sacrifice.

Good Hair, a profound and provocative documentary film by Chris Rock, claims that the hottest, most desired hair for extensions comes from India, one of the very poorest countries in the world. Hair is second to software in their export business.[13] In India, hair is seen as a sign of vanity and cutting it is a form of sacrifice, an offering to Hindu gods.

The hair is then auctioned, processed, wrapped in bundles, and exported to factories for further processing, then sent to places like Great Lengths, in Kansas City, Missouri, where it is inspected and sold to salons around the United States. When women want overall lengthening, the stylist needs to attach 260 bundles of hair to the scalp. This can cost up to $2800 and take five hours or more. First, their own hair is braided into tiny sections, then bundles of hair are attached to the braids, with the tight stitching resulting in significant pain for many women. Follow-up includes visiting the salon regularly for washing, conditioning, and tightening. The biggest investment is the hair, but the aftercare also requires a sizeable outlay of time and money.

Although African Americans spend the most on these hair products, the U.S. hair weave business has been dominated by Asians, especially Koreans. The African American community has yet to claim a strong part of the market themselves, but that appears to be changing. Despite significant barriers to their entry into the black hair care and weaving business, as many as 50 companies led by African American entrepreneurs are now successfully producing products specific to this market.[14] Some of these brands (Carol's Daughter, Dudley's Q, curlBOX, Huetiful) are well known; others are newer. They are making important progress in reclaiming the "brown-beauty conversation" and hopefully bringing some of the opportunities for job creation and profit-making into the African American community.

As indicated by the numbers above, hair is a big business—while it can drain people's money and other resources, it also can create them. In fact, the first African American woman millionaire was Madam C.J. Walker, who was born to slaves and orphaned by the age of six.[15] After having lost hair due to exposure to chemicals in her work environment and experiencing countless other life stressors, Madam Walker created a product to stimulate hair growth, "Wonderful Hair Grower." She then developed other products (a hair oil, a psoriasis treatment, and a hot comb with widely spaced teeth) more suited to thick or coarse hair and gradually began to market these products, called the Walker System, door to door in the southern and eastern parts of the United States. Next came the training of other women to sell the products and develop their own businesses as well as the creation of Leila College in Pittsburgh to train beauticians in her methods and products. Madam Walker not only became a millionaire, but she also launched countless other women into careers in the hair business. Along the way, she developed Walker Clubs, groups of her agents and employees to empower them to become successful in business but also active in their communities and charities promoting social and economic justice. Going from Sarah Breedlove, the daughter of sharecroppers, to a self-made millionaire and anti-lynching activist, Madam Walker left a large estate to charities including the NAACP.

Madam C.J. Walker's story is the American dream come true—a person overcoming adversity, committed to hard work and with a resilient attitude toward life who created a product and a business through which she could economically empower others and do good. Speaking of dreams, Madam Walker's inspiration for her hair growth stimulator came from a dream about an African hair product. May today's hair care entrepreneurs be as inspired to do good for others. And may they benefit from the knowledge we have today about toxicity of the chemicals we apply to our hair so the advances they make are safe and cause no further health risks.

The Economic Impact of the Proverbial "Bad Hair Day"

A "bad hair day" is no joke. In fact, hair care lines spend considerable time and money researching what makes a "good hair day," even employing Ivy League researchers to figure out the emotions underlying those favorite and very welcome days. As many as 25 percent of women report not wanting to leave the house on a bad hair day,[16] a term so frequently used that a Google search yields over 2,330,000,000 "hits" (as of November 2021). The same search for good hair day registers even more (4,690,000,000), including lots of products to promote good hair days.

After the economic recession that reduced U.S. discretionary spending in 2008, Procter & Gamble devoted a huge amount of research and advertising to the concept of the bad hair day. While hair care was still a priority for women, many saved by trading down to less expensive products or less frequent trips to the salon. To protect and develop their place in the market, P&G promised not only to wash and condition our hair, but also to make us feel better about life by getting rid of those annoying and disarming bad hair days.

First, the researchers used a survey of women's emotions to understand what a bad hair day meant to them, and then they used neuroscience, studying brainwaves as women looked at ads for hair products to see which held their attention. Employing a well-established psychological tool, the Positive and Negative Affect Schedule, and Yale psychology professor Marianne Lafrance to analyze the data, P&G found that women associated certain hair products with feeling hostile, nervous, or jittery and others with feeling excited, proud, or interested. Some women even reported feeling less hostile and nervous when they used certain products. LaFrance's earlier research had illustrated how bad hair affects self-esteem, increasing insecurities, self-doubt, and negative feelings. Based on this information, P&G developed their Pantene line, with new products, packaging, and advertising including a subsequent ad showing how "bad hair" affects a woman. Their approach seems to have worked. Pantene is now a significant brand in the P&G assortment of beauty products.

Marketing is critical even when products are popular and seen as a necessary part of routine grooming. The Pantene brand promotes "Strong Is Beautiful," having added film actress, producer, and philanthropist Priyanka Chopra to their Global Brand Ambassador program.[17] The ad campaign heralds her inner strength and beauty, suggesting that Pantene's products provide additional strength to hair so it can "endure the stressors it faces day in and day out." As one P&G marketing executive said regarding the benefit of research on the complicated relationship between women and hair and their hair care decisions, "the sky's the limit." And the sky may be the limit on what women are willing to spend for good hair—or even for one good hair day.

Hair Stories:
The Realities of Hair Today

CHAPTER 7

Hair and Me

"Ask a woman about her hair and you just might get the story of her whole life."—Elizabeth Benedict[1]

To be honest, despite my professional interest in how women use their hair to express deeper issues, when I started writing this book, I thought this was an issue for other people, not really for me. There were patients who expressed suicidal thoughts after a perm, color, or cut failed to deliver the look they wanted, and friends who spent what seemed to me inordinate amounts of time on their hair each day. And there were the many women I observed spending precious hours on Saturdays at salons trying to find the perfect look while I drove by on my way to take a hike. All those other women were tangled up in knots about their hair, but my hair was just my hair. Only now am I beginning to see how my hair projects some of the deeper issues in my life and reflects the choices I have made. It really is every woman's issue.

The "Pixie"

I wonder who I would be today if I hadn't had that short pixie cut I was known for during my formative childhood years.

I grew up in the 1950s, a member of the baby boomer generation, part of a large Irish-Catholic extended family in a small town in northwestern Connecticut. Both of my parents' families were hardworking, serious, and smart, with an underlying desire to make the world a better place—the old-fashioned pillars of the community. In high school, the occasional teacher would call me by my mother's maiden name rather than by my surname which, as tradition had it, was from my father. I desperately wanted to be seen as me, Margo Maine, as I knew myself. I was a feminist before I knew the word, wanting my own identity and power rather than riding the coattails of my family's positive image and reputation.

My parents both loved the outdoors and shared this gift with us, taking full advantage of our proximity to the Appalachian Trail and other great natural resources for outdoor activities. A family that worked hard and played hard, we were lucky enough to have a summer cottage on a family compound at a quiet and pristine lake nearby. To this day I find great solace in nature and in that water. Anyone who swims as much as I do has learned that swimming trumps a hairstyle any day of the week.

My mother was a kind-hearted, intelligent, and educated woman with an active lifestyle and a simple, low-maintenance approach to beauty—minimal make-up and hair long enough to pull back, permed around the ends, and in a ponytail during the summer so she could swim freely and not have to style it. She was comfortable in her own skin and a natural beauty. When I was little, she wanted my hair to be just as simple as hers. The "pixie" was in, and I was that pixie— except for the summer that my father cut my hair.

Every summer my dentist-dad became a part-time barber, using electric shears on my brothers to avoid driving into town for haircuts. A tradition soon emerged—he cut the hair of all the boys nearby, so those lazy, hazy, crazy days of summer would not be interrupted. One summer, when I was six or seven, my mom put me and my pixie cut in the lineup so she could avoid that trip to town as well. When my turn came, my dad was on auto pilot, and, before thinking about it, gave me just about the same cut as the boys—practically a buzz-cut, but with bangs! Fortunately, I was at an age when looking in the mirror was not a big part of my life. Still, this buzz-with-bangs was a powerful message: your hair is far less important than a good hike and swimming for hours every day. I really like that value system, and I still live by it. But even back then I could tell that the hair lessons I was learning were very different from what my friends with long hair or ringlets were absorbing from their families. Some girls did not even swim when they came to the lake to avoid messing up their hair! Or they swam straining to keep their head out of the water or wearing an ugly plastic bathing cap. Our differences were clear, and my hair was always wet.

By the time I was in fifth grade, my mother indulged my growing desire to conform to the styles girls my age were sporting. I wore my hair a little longer, with home perms and the usual fights about it being in my eyes. I know my mom did not enjoy spending hours curling my hair and putting smelly chemicals on it, but she recognized that leaving that pixie cut behind was an important rite of passage for me. Within a few years, by the mid–1960s, Vidal Sassoon transformed the world of hair with his very modern short cuts, liberating women from hours of hair care. In high school, inspired by Sassoon, I was back to short hair, although certainly edgier than that childhood pixie. Next, in keeping with the times and with my antiwar and activist politics, I grew my hair in college, and, except for a few years in my middle to late 20s, wore it shoulder length or longer for the next three decades.

"It looks horrible"

Although she always agreed with my politics, as time went by, my mother came to dislike my long, straight hair. In her later years, whenever I told her I was getting a haircut, she would shake her head and say, "Well, you're not getting your money's worth—it looks exactly the same all the time. It looks horrible." I still am not quite sure why she disliked my longer hair so much. Maybe she was just tired of it. Or, maybe, like many, she believed that, once women get into their 40s, they should no longer wear their hair long. I know she always preferred the neat and controlled look of short hair versus the loose flow of longer tresses, and she and my dad had both grown up in families that valued control. Could it be as simple as feeling she had lost her control over me when I grew my hair? Was it a symbolic loss of the earlier days and times in our family? A desire to go back to those lazy, hazy, crazy days of summer when we were all together, life was simpler, and my hair was short? One day, despite knowing that I was fighting a losing battle, I said, "Gee, I get compliments about my hair all the time. Everyone else seems to like it." Instantly, she replied, in an extremely uncharacteristic choice of words and harsh tone, "They're all sucking up to you—they want something from you. Only your mother tells you the truth about your hair."

It has taken me a while to figure out "the truth" about my hair. What my mother did not know was that this long, unchanging hair had a lot to do with her and with the transition I was going through as she aged. In fact, I did not recognize that at the time either. After a very active lifestyle, my mother was ill for the last 19 years of her life, almost dying several times, and many elders in my family had already passed on. I was navigating an exciting but challenging professional career and I desperately needed something to stay the same. Somehow, I felt my long, straight hair would help to ground me in an unpredictable time. My hair was kind of like a glacier—on the outside it looked the same, but inside my head, and in my heart, a lot of losses, turmoil, and changes were taking place. The reflection in the mirror helped me to keep everything from changing too fast.

Those harsh words stuck with me. "Only your mother tells you the truth about your hair." So now she is dead, and guess what? My hair is a lot shorter, and I get more compliments than before. Plus, I really like it. Maybe she was right all along, but for so many years, I wanted her out of my hair.

"The truth about your hair"

The more I think of my own experience and talk to other women, the more I appreciate the significant role hair can play in our individuation process, the journey to knowing and defining ourselves as separate people and as women.

Prior to telling me "the truth," my mother had her own major metamorphosis with her hair, and not by choice. She had kept her hair in the same style for her entire adult life—it looked pretty and was low-maintenance enough to work for her. But that all changed suddenly. When she was 71 and I was 34, my mother—that active woman who took rigorous hikes a few times each week, swam every day in the summer, and never shied from a physical challenge—fell on the stairs and broke her neck.

After her emergency admission to a major medical center, the neurosurgical resident had shaved my mother's head to drill her skull, preparing it for the traction apparatus necessary to prevent paralysis and stabilize her condition until she was ready for a cervical fusion. I was totally unprepared when I walked into her hospital room and saw the top of her head bald, with some sad, stringy hair left around the nape of her neck, and bright red blood oozing out of the holes drilled into her skull. The neurosurgeon was kind and compassionate, explaining the what and the why of every step they were taking, but all I could focus on was this shaved head and the dripping blood. I wanted to run out of the room and away from this image of my mother. Seeing her incapacitated was hard enough, but the bald head made it so much worse. I had never imagined seeing her without her salt-and-pepper, neatly-styled hair. Despite feeling overwhelmed, I stayed with my mother who remained her stoic self—but then again, she could not see this bald and bloody head. Maybe seeing it would have rattled her strength the way it rattled mine.

First thing the next day, I was on the phone with my hair stylist, desperately asking for advice about my mother's hair. It seemed like the biggest problem, but, of course, it was truly minuscule in light of what we were facing with delicate spine surgery and intense physical rehabilitation that would dominate the next year and change our lives immeasurably. Like so many in that field, Carol is always ready to help a client get through an unexpected life event so she readily agreed to come to the hospital that day to see what solution she could offer to my mother's hair. She ended up suggesting that we have the nurses shave the rest. That made total sense, and, before I could blink, it was done.

Still, despite recognizing her fall as a game-changer for all of us, I wanted my mother's hair to look the same as it had for years. That would have eased the shock of her aging, her fragility, and the pending transformation of our roles as she would need me in a way she never had before. When her hair grew back, she chose to keep it super short—she loved the look and it suited her. Then, as time passed, and it was more difficult for my mother to get to a salon, I ended up buying electric shears and being her stylist, so now I was keeping her hair short. This role reversal happens for many mothers and daughters and brings up lots of emotions.

Hair is definitely a family affair, and our early hair stories are clearly imposed by others, with my pixie and the identity issues it initiated as my mother's choice for me. As a little girl, I was a bit of a tomboy, always trying to keep up with my brothers, cousins, and their friends. If I had been raised by a mother who valued a real "girly" look, I might have had a very different experience, with less outdoor play and less connection to nature and more time focusing on appearance. I am so glad I had a mother like her.

As we grow up, we can create more of our own style and the narrative that explains it. And as years pass and we develop more perspective, we may realize how much our hair represents a reactive versus a proactive process. Clearly those early hair experiences, as the pixie who could swim for hours without having to spend time on snarls, tangles, and knots at the end of the day, helped to define my life in positive ways.

The Lessons of Hair

Now I realize that the pixie was not only a short cut: it was actually a *shortcut* through some of the pressures of being a girl, allowing me to be less invested in the traditional female pursuits of beauty, and it may have ignited my passion to help women accept themselves as they are. I escaped the lure of our beauty sick culture[2] that prizes external looks above internal values, drains our energy and makes the image in the mirror more important than the inner self. That pixie cut may in fact have launched my career as a psychologist helping women figure out who they are and who they want to be, separate from their bodies, their weight, their appearance, and the unrelenting sociocultural pressures to meet the current cultural standard of beauty.

Those lessons I learned about hair during those formative years have been put to good use. I knew from early on, despite later wanting to be a bit more like the other girls, that I was freer from the oppression of worrying about my hair and appearance than most of my peers—and I feel very fortunate about that. But, as Jung suggests, for women, hair always reflects deep-rooted issues: so, even for me, despite a low-maintenance daily routine, my hair is not just hair.

For years I have joked "the only fake thing about me is my hair color." But when you are in the business of helping other people become more real, being fake is not a good joke or something to be proud of. Despite my advocacy for women aging naturally and embracing our bodies, I cover up that natural gray. I pride myself on how I "walk the talk" and never expect my patients or my friends to face things that I have run away from. I know who I am and readily show that person to the world. But, years ago when I was applying for a passport, I could not answer that trick question about hair color. I am rarely at a loss for words so this stopped me in my tracks and was one of those "aha" moments about the meaning hair can have. This is how it happened.

After I gave my passport application to her, the clerk looked it over briefly and handed it back to me, saying, "You didn't check off your hair color."

Embarrassed, I replied with a bit of panic in my voice, "But I don't know my hair color."

She looked at me, baffled, irritated, or both, and, with clear authority, said, "Brown."

I wonder if she saw my spirits sag. I sure felt them plummet. The answer about the color of my hair was simple, but it surprised me. I remember standing there, disappointed that my hair could be so simply described, as it felt like much more of a mystery to me, and "brown" does not sound very complex. Thinking back now, I realize I never really have known my hair color. When I was younger, it was dark but had a lot of red highlights, especially in the summer. People often commented on that, while others used to say they loved how black my hair was. My hair felt like some sort of chameleon, taking on different colors for different people. When my hairdresser started to color it, she always blended three or four different colors, all with jazzy names and not one of them "brown." To be honest, I really, truly have never known what color my hair is—even before we were coloring it to hide the gray! How could I know so much about myself and not know this?

My entire life I was told I looked just like my aunt and god-mother who was gray by the age of 30 and died when I was about five. My first gray hair appeared when I was 16, and every time I saw another, I worried that the same thing would happen to me. I loved my memories of my aunt and everything I knew about her, but I did not want her gray hair. And I certainly did not want to die young. By the time I was 30, my hairdresser was covering the gray with henna, gradually shifting to less natural treatments as the uninvited, genetically predestined gray slowly increased. So when I was asked about my hair color that memorable day, I had no clue what box to check off—me the nature girl and body image expert, the one who helps everyone else understand their deep, dark secrets and prides herself on pushing forward in personal growth. I simply had no clue: black, brown, red, auburn, gray? I knew I wasn't blond, but that was as far as I could get.

As I have thought about it further, I realize that on a deeper level the color of my hair was really a tapestry of emotions and family losses and connections, including a desire to have my own head of hair, not my aunt's. And despite how closely linked my feelings about my hair are to my aunt's legacy, no one else in the family may have ever been aware of this, because our associations to our hair are so deep, often unconscious, and usually unsaid. "Brown" fails to capture the color of all those emotions. Although my hair color may have been coming out of boxes for many years, it certainly did not fit into a box on that form.

I can see now how my hair has been a way to express autonomy and separateness. The desires to have my own head of hair and my own identity, to stay connected to my aunt and my heritage in ways other than hair color, to not look old when I was still young, and, most of all, to not die young, are big parts of my inability to pin down my hair color. I must admit that covering the gray for all these years undermines my general low-maintenance, natural approach to beauty and body image, but that 90 minutes every month at the salon seems a fair trade. Like many other women, I have developed a trusting and deep relationship with my hairstylist Carol—she is an important and special person in my life.

As for most women, something has been happening on the top of my head. While my life may be a journey of authenticity in so many dimensions, I still do not know my hair color. My hair has been that Rorschach, the projective expression of who I am, who I have been, and who I want to be. Yes, my hair tells a story, too, and understanding this story helps me to understand my life in deeper and productive ways. Hair is every woman's issue.

CHAPTER 8

Our Mothers: Our Hair

"Both mothers and daughters often regard each other as reflections of themselves and consequently look at each other with a level of scrutiny that they otherwise reserve for themselves."—Deborah Tannen[1]

"Mom" and hair are tangled together into one great knot for most women. It is as if hair is some sort of umbilical cord that keeps us connected to that life source forever.

We learn so much about being a woman from our mothers. From the moment we emerge from the womb, how they feel about their bodies and their appearance colors how they respond to ours. Body image, or, in this case, "hair image," is never an individual phenomenon, as mothers' feelings, beliefs, and behaviors about their own hair create their approach to their daughters.

Early in our lives, hair care and rituals become a laboratory classroom full of lessons that can last a lifetime. Out of this "hairy" intergenerational hand-me-down system, some hair stories are good and some are bad, but others are just plain *ugly*. Young or old, mother or daughter, the topic of hair can ignite a small spark that turns into a major flare-up in no time. Hair is definitely a shared experience.

In *Me, My Hair and I: 27 Women Untangle an Obsession*,[2] mother-daughter stories appear throughout the book, along with stories about sisters and grandmothers. Competition and control are frequent themes. The bios of the 27 women writers are peppered with descriptions of their "award-winning" and "best-selling" works and countless great accomplishments. But they too are obsessed with and conflicted and often unhappy about their hair.

A Linguist Takes a Look

A woman's hair story is always rooted in her family. Important battles for control and independence may be waged over a head of hair, as girls use their hair to express identity and individuation issues starting early and proceeding throughout childhood, adolescence, and adulthood. *Hair tells a story*—and a multigenerational family story more often than not.

The noted linguist Deborah Tannen has written extensively about the underlying meanings and motivations in human conversations. Her work includes an intriguing book about mother-daughter communication, *You're Wearing That? Understanding Mothers and Daughters in Conversation.* As she interviewed women for that book, three themes emerged as the primary areas of mother-daughter conflict: hair, clothes, and weight. Hair not only led the pack for frequency of criticisms, but Tannen also described hair comments as the most unnerving. These "metamessages of caring and criticism"[3] start with a mother expressing caring and end with the daughter feeling criticized. Tannen describes the daughters also feeling wounded because the mothers' concerns about their hair ignored other more important and pressing issues in their lives. Once more, it is never just about hair. Instead, these conversations are always about hurt feelings, misunderstandings, broken connections, and personal power. Hair can tell many stories.

According to Tannen's linguistic analysis of her interviews, mothers tend to feel deeply obligated and responsible to improve their daughters' lives. She sees this as a basic maternal motivation. Knowing how harshly our culture judges the appearance of girls of all ages, mothers desperately want to protect their daughters and to help them to look their best—to be attractive and sexy, but not to an extreme. Because puberty ushers in some major physical differences with girls developing breasts, adding body fat and curves with less facial hair and more head hair, Tannen conceptualizes hair as a secondary sex characteristic. Most cultures do in fact link hair with sexuality and attractiveness, so teaching daughters about how to manage their hair is a critical life skill. As Tannen says, "hair is an essential element in this sexual equation."[4] No wonder hair sparks so much mother-daughter conflict and connection.

My interviews with women echoed Tannen's impressions in many ways. In fact, no woman who shared her hair story with me left her mother out of it—"Mom" was always tangled up in their relationship to her hair, some more dramatically than others but always there. Many women describe their mothers imposing a particular style or keeping their hair short throughout their childhood for their convenience, like my mother did. No surprise, this can lead to a fierce desire for daughters to take charge of their own hair, wrestling for decades with the remnants of this mother-daughter tension. Others report that their mothers punished them for not combing their hair and keeping it neat by having it cut very short. As adults, they have used long hair as a powerful statement of autonomy. And others relate that their mothers demanded long hair, or straightened hair, that required a great deal of tending and discomfort, with Mom insisting that this was just "the price of beauty" to their little girls. Women of color have especially complicated relationships with their mothers and their hair due to today's biased beauty norms that idealize the Caucasian standard of straight hair. (See Chapter 13.)

"Sometimes I think that not having to worry about your hair anymore is the secret upside of death."
—NORA EPHRON[5]

Hair-Raising Experiences

Parenting always causes the pain of one's own childhood to resurface and hair is one more arena for this to occur. The relationship with a mother and other important caregivers can be deeply affected by the caregiver's feelings or attitudes toward the child's hair, by the time it requires to get it looking presentable and by family traditions, rules, and expectations regarding appearance and management of hair. At some point, often between the ages of three and six, girls express a desire to control their hair, even cutting it themselves with their child-friendly, dull scissors. Parents' reactions to these moments can be powerful, as many have difficulty simply recognizing this as a positive or normal step toward individuation and growth. Instead, the new, odd haircut shocks and embarrasses them, representing a loss of the image they had hoped their child would maintain as well as a tangible loss of control over this little being. Nightmares about what the future holds are common, as the child makes more and more steps toward self-determination, all started by a few snips of the scissors.

One woman described a very loving family, but she was still baffled that her otherwise supportive parents called her "mattress-head" throughout her childhood. Her hair was thick and hard to manage, very different from the texture of her mother's and other family members. Her mother would say she had "enough hair to fill a mattress," thus launching her into an ambivalent relationship with her hair until midlife when she finally accepted and embraced her natural tresses. When I met her, I admired her wavy, thick, chestnut hair, never guessing the pain it had caused her for decades before she came to accept it. I saw a nicely styled head of hair on a wonderful new friend, not what she saw in the mirror.

On the positive side, some of the most soothing memories of childhood involve mothers' combing and fussing over their daughters' hair. Mary Catherine Bateson speaks of these special moments with her mother calmly stroking and caring for her long hair.[6] Bateson was the only daughter of two world-renowned anthropologists, Margaret Mead and Gregory Bateson, and they traveled the globe together, sometimes living in very primitive quarters. She described the 20 minutes her mother spent combing and braiding her tangled hair each morning as the most intimate time they shared. Most of us have some memory traces of lying on a grandmother's or mother's lap, with gentle hands caressing our hair. Whether our hair is long or short, our caretakers' hands tend to be drawn to it like a magnet. Those moments can give the ultimate comfort for both the caresser and the caressed. In contrast, some mothers struggle with their reactions to their children's hair. When the child's hair is radically different from their own, mothers feel especially inept at managing this unsung aspect of a parent's job.

These hair-raising experiences include embarrassment if the child does not have much hair during the first few years and a desire to make them more attractive, even to color their children's hair at young ages. One mother of two young children said: "I am so tempted to start lightening my son's hair—it was so blond, and I loved it, but now, he's only three and it's getting darker. And my daughter's hair is so much darker than I want it to be. I really have always wanted my kids to be blond—this is really hard for me. I know I could really mess up my kids if I did this, but if I were a different kind of person, I would go ahead and start coloring their hair anyway."

Families can easily and unintentionally create undue self-consciousness by calling attention to their children's hair or making it into a major project requiring time, techniques, and products to make it right.

The "Roots"

As Lindsey discussed her mother's approach to hair, we both saw some "roots" to her own relationship with her hair.

Lindsey's mother had had a tortuous relationship with her hair. Throughout her childhood, her own mother (Lindsey's grandmother) had kept it very long, down to her buttocks, in elaborate, time-consuming braids. Her mother told Lindsey that she always felt like a "doll or a girl in a costume," and to no surprise, as soon as she was in charge of her own life, she cut it short and kept it that way—until she started pulling it out.

Self-induced hair loss, called trichotillomania, is often compared to other obsessive behaviors like nail-biting and picking at one's skin and can result in large areas of baldness. For some people, this condition comes and goes, secondary to other stressors in their lives. (More on hair loss in Chapter 10.)

By the time Lindsey was 10, her mother had started to wear a wig all the time. She spent considerable cash on human hair wigs, always had more than one, and took elaborate care of them, bringing one to the stylist and wearing the other, so she never had to sit around the salon and wait. Her mother was in many ways an unconventional woman living a very conventional suburban stay-at-home mother/ corporate wife lifestyle. Looks were important, but she refused to devote much time to their pursuit, so this worked for her.

Lindsey's mother tended to be very critical of her only daughter, demanding that she pull her hair back, to wear a look that did not fit how Lindsey wanted to see herself. With her own investment in and reliance on her wigs, her mother had little to teach Lindsey about hair and how to manage it or express herself through it. Decades later, Lindsey's hair is very important to her, and despite their different approaches, as she tells me the story of her hair and her mother's, she finds some common ground between them. Lindsey does not like to fuss with her hair, wants a style that works, so like her mother, she will spend a lot of time and money up-front on a style so she does not have to fuss each day. This no-fuss style still requires considerable effort and planning, however, in terms of color, products, and keeping her hair the right length and in the right condition. She has searched for a hairdresser who understands her needs, and at one point, she had two different stylists in two different cities. Insisting on getting her needs recognized by her stylist has been empowering to her, indirectly helping her to set better boundaries with her mother, but, oddly enough, for years she gravitated to having her hair always just long enough to pull back, as her mother always insisted.

Aging, Illness and the Mother-Daughter Hair Dance

Jackie, in her early 30s, and her hair have been on quite a journey. And this journey intersects with her mother, her mother's values and feelings about hair, and the dramatic changes life brings when we are the least prepared. As she says, "Growing up, my mom's hair was very important to her. Following her lead, my hair became very important to me."

Jackie's earliest memories include constantly hearing "how cute my blond curls were" from pretty much everyone she met. For years, she had a lot invested in the look of her hair—its blond color, natural wave, and long length, stating that, at a young age, she had internalized the cultural message "women should have long hair." She still remembers how much she hated the one short haircut she had as a child. Ever since, she has consistently expressed her femininity through her long hair, enjoying a connection with her mother through what she describes as a shared fixation on their hair.

Suddenly—almost overnight—all the investment in their hair disappeared. Jackie's mother was diagnosed with a rare form of cancer. Because little research had been done on this particular cancer, the road ahead of them has been unclear since her diagnosis, but it has changed everything. When chemotherapy caused her mother's hair to begin to fall out, Jackie and her father lovingly shaved her mother's head. She describes it as "a very surreal experience for all of us. As it turns out, my mom's hair doesn't mean as much to her as she or anyone else thought. Today, she walks around us with no hair, no wig, and no hat. She walks around bald, and I see the strongest woman I know. Hair doesn't seem to matter in the end. Life and love do."

Several years since her mother's diagnosis, Jackie is still surprised with the transformation she and her mother have experienced when it comes to the importance of hair. For both, their long, flowing hair had been a way to display their femininity, to garner attention, and to feel attractive and sexy. Hair had been the focal concern when it came to their appearance and self-confidence and the trusted answer to all those questions women struggle with about whether they are going to be noticed, admired, respected, and valued by men and by other women. Now that variable is missing for Jackie's mother. Seeing her mother without her hair allowed Jackie to see the real person underneath and to see herself for the first time as well. Both mother and daughter have been transformed and have a deeper appreciation for life, for family, and for everything they have right now. Hair seems far less important—an accessory rather than a core asset.

Oddly enough, cancer and other serious illnesses can free us from burdens that we had not recognized we were carrying. For

Jackie and her mother, the meaning of their hair had limited their experience of life. Her mother's hair loss ended up being a gift to both of them.

"Conscious Hair-Raising"

Raising children is the hardest job known to (wo)man. Especially today, in the era of instant gratification, instant distraction, and instant competition, parents have endless concerns and worries. Bullying is prominent on that radar screen, as we read countless heartbreaking stories of its tragic outcomes. Teasing about hair can be part of a bullying campaign, targeted at vulnerable kids, especially if they look different due to race, ethnicity, class, or a physical characteristic. Instantly visible, hair can be a lightning rod of self-doubt or it can be a secure crown of confidence. Parents need to watch their reaction to their children's hair and be sure they are not setting them up for feeling different or inadequate. Sensing parents' unconditional love is a great immunizer against the toxins of today's culture.

"Conscious hair-raising" (my own term) can be an important ingredient in children's self-esteem and self-confidence. These two stories are examples of thoughtful mothers preparing their daughters for some of the inevitable challenges of childhood by creating pride and confidence instead of shame and inadequacy when it comes to the topic of hair.

Denise has a preschool daughter, Elizabeth, whom she loves and enjoys immensely. When I met Denise, she had streaks of pink hair. With joy in her face and laughter in her voice, she explained that pink was her daughter's favorite color and she thought it would be fun to have pink hair. It sure was—for both of them. Elizabeth seemed to intuitively understand that Denise was celebrating her love for her by sporting pink hair. She just loved Denise's hair and their shared passion for pink.

After a few months of all this hair-related fun, Elizabeth came home from preschool with lice in her beautiful, thick, long, wavy hair.

Combing it out for hours was not doing the job of getting rid of these annoying pests, and Denise was afraid of creating some painful memories for Elizabeth. She did what had to be done and cut the infested hair, but made this into a fun ritual, rather than mourning for her daughter's lost waves. Denise was sad to give Elizabeth her first real haircut—those long curls had been growing since she was a baby and had already become a trademark for this little girl. Denise knew she would miss running her hands through that hair as she held her or rocked her to sleep. She handled those feelings of loss herself without sharing them with Elizabeth. She wanted Elizabeth to feel good about herself no matter what her hair looked like and not sense her disappointment about having to cut Elizabeth's hair.

Everyone at Elizabeth's school and in her neighborhood noticed this change and people were constantly asking about her shorter hair. With no shame whatsoever, Elizabeth would proudly announce "we had bugs." Denise is hoping to instill this non-shaming attitude in all her interactions with her daughter and is thrilled that her daughter laughs instead of cries about her hair and the reasons for its new length. Before long, this proud and happy little soul had started a haircut club, initiating a movement toward shorter hair among her preschool peers! Denise's conscious hair-raising will serve Elizabeth well in life.

Dianna, an accomplished woman in her early 30s and a first-time mother of a baby girl, has also committed to what I describe as conscious hair-raising. Her earliest memories are of Saturday mornings when she was four or five when conflicts about her natural hair began to blossom. Her mother would wash her hair, then braid it when it was wet. If it was allowed to air dry, a comb would never penetrate that thick, nappy texture. All she remembers is heat and pain to get her hair straight: hot combs on the stove and grease that would burn her scalp, in a mother-daughter ritual fraught with the literal pain of a burning scalp. She is determined to never "relax" her baby's hair and instead to learn how to work with her natural curl.

Dianna sees the African American community of women as still caught up in self-hatred about skin tone and hair and desperately wants to protect her daughter from this. As a young mother, she constantly hears the conversations about little girls' hair that start off with "What are we going to do with her hair?" After years of insecurities related to her hair and resentment of the time and expense of trying to manage it, Dianna has answered that question: "I was always deathly afraid of having a daughter. I didn't know what kind of hair she would have and knew it would take so much time to learn how to bring out the beauty of kinky hair. I don't want to pass along my self-hatred. She's still an infant but I have vowed to never straighten her hair. I'm going to let her love it, instead of believing there is something wrong with it."

Dianna is determined to love her daughter's natural hair so that her daughter will love it too. She does not have to hand down the tradition she knew as a child. Instead, she can give the love and care she received without the tensions and insecurities about hair that came with those mother-daughter rituals.

Fathers: An Afterthought or More?

Whenever women talk about their hair, mothers figure prominently—they really are on center-stage in these conversations. Fathers are at best an afterthought if they are mentioned at all. Occasionally women have described that their fathers liked hair a certain way—usually long due to traditional views about women and/or religious beliefs. Many felt the need to look feminine in the way their father preferred, but most of their thoughts about hair are colored more by what they believe other women expect. Some women raised in conservative religions were expected to have long hair and they felt caught between their fathers' traditions and their own wishes and new relationships. One woman balanced these tensions by growing her hair long to please her father, then cutting it to please her husband, but giving it to Locks of Love for cancer patients. Then she would repeat the pattern. She could offset her guilt for going against her father's wishes as long as someone else benefited.

CHAPTER 9

"Hair doesn't get fat":
Hair and Body Image

"Hair is a woman's glory."—Maya Angelou[1]

Before I finished introducing the reasons I was writing about women and their hair, Laura, a very attractive woman who nonetheless struggles with body image and weight concerns, blurted, "Hair doesn't get fat—I have to have it long and blond—a way to stand out but something to hide behind as well. It protects me. I think of cutting it off, but I never will. I can feel good about it even if I hate my body."

Laura is a single woman in a highly visible and stressful job in a very competitive male-dominated field. She has little extra time and tends to be frugal with her finances as she plans for her future, knowing hers may be the only income and retirement savings she will have when that time comes. Although she spends money carefully, her hair is a top priority in her budget, as it promises a safe feeling in contrast to the other aspects of her body image. That long blond hair is like an insurance policy that she can count on when nothing else feels good.

Laura lost her dad when she was only 14 and her mother worked hard to provide for her family but was constantly critical of her own appearance and weight. As an eating disorder expert, I see many women who avoid deep or painful feelings by focusing on appearance, and it seems Laura's mother did just that. Thus, despite many admirable qualities, she was not a great role model when it came to body image, that critical issue for her teenage daughter. This launched Laura into years of chronic and severe dieting. After landing in the emergency room with cardiac issues and dehydration, Laura had to admit to having an eating disorder and to commit to eating better and gaining some needed but unwelcome pounds. Since this weight gain, her hair has become even more important to her. As she said, "hair doesn't get fat."

For Laura, hair is her trademark, legitimizing her as a woman in the masculine culture of her work world. It allows her a sense of control that she does not have with any other part of her body. She likes it, even on the many days she hates herself. In Laura's mind, her distinctive long blond mane makes up for gaining a small amount of weight, so she looks thin but not emaciated. Laura is now approaching 50, and her hair is a connection to her youth, as it has not changed despite the number of pounds on the scale and candles on the birthday cake.

Hair and Self-Image

Hair is a powerful ingredient in a woman's self-image—and it can be both controlled and transformed easily. Many women echoed this sentiment: "I consider it the most important statement about my overall look. If my hair is OK, I can cope better with my struggles about my body and my weight. So it's very important to me and a bad hair day is a serious problem."

Sheryl shared this: "My hair is one of the few parts of my body that I've always liked. When I was a child and adolescent, I was fat. Everyone would still tell me I was pretty and would tell me how pretty my hair was. So hair felt safe to me. Even when I've had a haircut or a color I didn't like at the moment, I could usually have it fixed pretty quickly. I've always liked having the ability to change it on a whim—wear it short, long, curly, straight—depending on my mood, where I am in my life, relationships, etc. It's my head decoration. And it has helped me a lot to make peace with my body."

Another woman described how her hair gave her important feelings about her sexuality or attractiveness that her body never delivered. "As a teen, I took great pride in my waist-length, thick, dark brown hair. I am petite and recall feeling that my breasts were too small (a size I am grateful to have now), so my hair, to me, was my femininity, my voluptuousness, you might say."

In contrast to the constantly changing female body as we go through menstrual cycles, pregnancies, menopause and all that these normal lifecycles do to our bodies, hair changes less, sometimes less visibly, but changes later in most cases. As Melissa explained in her *hair story*, "At 64, overall, I don't turn heads anymore, but my hair does, so I love it and truly treasure it."

Many women have told me that hair seems to be a safer area to share positive feedback and compliments with each other and that it seems to evoke less jealousy, envy, or competition. Somehow expressing themselves through their hair, even making a dramatic statement, feels less disruptive to their relationships with other women. I am not sure why this is, but having heard many women say this, it has begun to ring true to me.

"Your hair looks great":
The Ultimate Double Bind

Those four words, "Your hair looks great," have immeasurable power. Every woman wants to hear them. Unfortunately, these words are also the ultimate double bind. For Laura, Melissa, Sheryl, and many other women, their hair evokes many positive feelings about themselves. But for others, the words "Your hair looks great," so deeply desired, come with a heavy price.

Catherine's *hair story* illustrates the dramatic cost extracted by those four simple words. She does important work in an important field. An accomplished feminist advocate with a no-nonsense approach to life, Catherine appears professional but warm at the same time. When she described to me how complicated her morning hair routine is, I was shocked. Although I liked the look of this strong, centered woman's hair, I had no clue the meaning it held and the energy it took from her.

My morning routine centers around my hair. Washing, conditioning, and towel-drying are the easy part. Then it gets complicated. There's the professional grade hair dryer, clips, three different brushes, and the delicate choice of which hair care product combinations to use given the weather report: humectant, anti-humectant, curl enhancer, straightening balm, crème with silk groom, texturizing gel, shine emollient, thickening mist, volumizing tonic, Moroccan hair oil, and flexible-but-firm-hold hair spray. Then I go about my morning and come back again to the mirror and the hair dryer to add finishing touches and products. The whole process takes about 45 minutes. "Can't you just dry your hair once?" my partner asks. Nope. Round two is important, otherwise my bangs may have rearranged or worse—frizzed—in the rushing of the morning.

Despite the work it takes—or because of it—Catherine's "hair looks great." It looks so consistently great that some are jealous, and many others have asked if it is a wig! Great hair, however, comes with a price, as we see in Catherine's story. Gradually, Catherine has come to understand that her feelings about her hair are deeply rooted in her identity and family relationships. This insight has been nothing less than life-changing, eventually allowing her to invest far less in her hair.

Like Laura's, the story of Catherine's hair and the degree to which it assumed power in her life has much to do with the messages her mother delivered to her from her earliest days. According to all reports and photos, Catherine was nearly bald as an infant but still her mother was always doing something to her hair. As soon as she had any hair, it was stiffly curled on top of her head with Dippity Do. Later, her mother employed curling irons, perms, and other tortuous methods, never accepting its natural texture or waves. By the time Catherine was 13, her mother was coloring her hair, not liking its progression from blond to brown. Their harried interactions culminated in this unforgettable quote: "With hair like that, I'm ashamed to call you my daughter."

Catherine has worked hard to reclaim her hair, gradually letting go of more and more of the tools and tricks her mother passed on to her. As an adult, she realized she was being as critical of her hair (and herself) as her mother had been for years. So she is taking it back to its natural color, walking in the rain, even if her hair is likely to frizz, and allowing someone to hug her despite the potential to muss her perfect coif. Although they were a long time coming, these steps have been liberating for Catherine. Coming to peace with her hair and no longer battling its natural tendencies has been a way to make peace with herself, to begin to give up some of her self-criticism and perfectionism. Being more accepting of her hair has allowed her to be kinder and gentler to herself, once more proving the role of hair in a woman's psyche and soul.

Like the rest of us, Catherine, regardless of her many strengths, lives in an image-based consumer culture that never tells a woman she is good enough as is. And this consumer-based economy is always selling one more thing to answer the questions it forces on us about our self-worth. In an era of unprecedented opportunities for women, we experience tremendous pressures to get ahead and, far too often, appearance seems to be the ticket.

Hair is so visible, so easily changed and "perfected" that having the best head of hair may seem to be the answer to all the questions contemporary women face. Countless products are marketed to women to alter their natural hair. Color, texture, volume, curl, and frizz are constant concerns. When I complimented a friend on her hair recently, she instantly replied, "I only used three products today." (That was three products in addition to shampoo and conditioner, a dryer and a curling rod, by the way!) Even when we get it "right," we cannot take credit; instead, we attribute compliments to a product we bought or a process done to us.

Literally and figuratively, we pay a great price to hear the words "Your hair looks great." And we seem to keep on paying. Greta, in her 80s, calls her hair "my crowning glory" but explains that a lifetime of compliments about her hair has exacted its toll. As she approaches 87 years of age, she stopped coloring her hair only in the few weeks prior to our interview. She explains that "compliments can become a burden" and they had for her. Greta felt constant pressure to keep her hair looking "lovely," as strangers and friends alike paid so much attention to it. Throughout her life, wherever she went, compliments about her hair were often the icebreakers, so her hair seemed essential to her social standing and to her identity. Early into this decision to stop coloring her hair, Greta hopes she can maintain this resolve but worries how others will react and what will replace those constant compliments. Her *hair story* shows us how important this issue is, no matter what age or life stage a woman is navigating.

"Einstein was always looking for a unifying principle for the universe. I think anxiety about hair is the unifying principle."
—DIANE SAWYER[2]

The Good Hair Day

To so many women, hair is a reliable barometer of their mood and the tone their day will take. How their hair goes, their day goes.

Johanna, a highly accomplished professional woman with a successful business, an expert in her field with a TED talk on her resume, still feels her hair affects the quality of every day of her life.

> When my hair is looking "good" (to my liking) it helps me to feel more confident and attractive, therefore I give it the power to project both of those qualities. I feel strong and ready for anything that comes my way.
>
> A "good hair day" has the power to boost my mood just the same as a "bad hair day" can depress my mood. When I perceive my hair to look "bad"— when it won't do what I want—an irritability can set in that is then there for me to have to manage the rest of the day. These feelings get stirred up whenever I see my reflection and I have to work consciously to manage them so I can stay above them.
>
> When I am not in the public eye or in my professional persona, I love not paying any attention to my hair and letting it be whatever "mess" it might be. I'm not in a mode of caring whether I look attractive, but more into being relaxed and releasing tension and cares. I love those days.

As a feminist, I dream of a time when our culture recognizes the worth, contributions and power of women and no longer sees them as "less than" men. When that day comes, "good hair days" and "bad hair days" can cease to exist. Every day women will feel empowered and equal, no matter what is happening on top of their heads.

CHAPTER 10

Hair Today, Gone Tomorrow

"Hair remains a curiously vulnerable repository of power. It grows inexplicably and imperceptibly, with the legless movement of a snake; when it disappears, it takes with it all of the brawn it once bestowed."—Diane Simon[1]

Hair is like a cover story—literally a headline. As with any other headline, you need to keep reading to grasp its truth. When people think of Dolly Parton, most envision that full head of blond hair curling around and adding a couple of inches of height to her petite frame. In fact, that hair is not hers—it is a temporary loan. She has worn wigs since she was 19 years old and is never seen publicly without one. Her hair is very fine, not easy to style and brown—not blond.

Wearing a wig is far easier than spending long hours at a hair salon and gives a more predictable result. With a supply of a dozen wigs on hand, she continues to wear them because "I don't want someone to see me and be disappointed.... What they're seeing reflects the phony that I am." Dolly doesn't see herself as a natural beauty and thinks she looks best this way: "Part of the magic is that I look so totally artificial but I am so totally real."[2] Her words are a great reminder: hair always tells a story and even fake hair can tell the story of a very real person.

While hair tells a story, its absence does too. To this day, when women shave their heads or cut their hair dramatically short, they are seen as making powerful statements of ownership and defiance. When a lesbian sports a "butch" look, most see this as a sign of rejection of traditional femininity. Bald monks or saints are seen as strong enough to abstain from worldly pleasures, while we tend to associate a skinhead's baldness with aggression.

Involuntary Hair Loss

Hair tells a story, but involuntary hair loss is a totally different story and a particularly painful experience for women. Consequently, women's hair restoration is a rapidly growing market, ranging from chemical products and processes to hair replacement surgeries, wigs, and weaves. A Google search of "women and hair loss" brings up 5,420,000,000 entries (as of December 18, 2021). Surprisingly, up to 40 percent of hair loss sufferers are women who literally "cover up" rather than expose the pain they feel about this. Hair and hair loss present endless opportunities to "big business" while simultaneously draining women's psychic energy. In fact, the United States spends more than $3.5 billion annually on hair loss solutions but 99 percent of these products will not help most of the consumers who buy them.[3]

The loss of hair, such a central element in body image, and so evident to the world, can be a devastating experience for women— and one that silences so many of them. For men, hair loss is not usually a welcome stage in life, but it is not as disarming as it is for women. Our images of success and social status include bald and balding men, but not bald and balding women. While men may even be proud of their baldness, women tend to be deeply ashamed and to avoid talking about hair loss with anyone, even close friends or medical providers.

Annie, in her mid–30s, confided that a friend she has known since first grade has worn wigs for years but has never talked about it or the reasons why, causing many an awkward silence. The wig has changed from time to time, but Annie is hesitant to acknowledge that she notices this or to compliment her friend's appearance. She is not even comfortable mentioning things as simple as her own hair appointments. They have shared pretty much everything over the years, from the dramas of middle school to their first sexual experiences and now to their lives as married professionals starting families, but the wigs and whatever led to them have created a wall of silence that Annie has never challenged. She senses that any mention of hair would shatter her friend and perhaps their friendship.

As hormonal shifts begin in midlife, hair begins to thin and grow more slowly—just a natural part of the aging process. As many as two-thirds of postmenopausal women experience some hair loss—either thinning or bald spots. This "normal" type of hair loss, called androgenetic alopecia, is similar for men and women although the pattern of loss varies.[4]

A receding hairline with thinning and balding on top is standard for men. For women, hair gradually thins at the part line, with diffuse hair loss radiating across the scalp from the top of the head. In contrast to men, women's hairlines rarely recede, and women rarely become bald. The term androgenetic reflects the biological process underlying hair loss. "Anagen," the growing phase of the hair follicle, gradually shortens over time and the time between the hair shedding and the new anagen phase lengthens. Women's hair growth is slower, and lush, thick, pigmented hairs disappear with shorter, thinner, non-pigmented hairs taking their place. While the physical process may be similar, the experience and meaning of hair loss is more gendered. Some women choose to wear their baldness as a sign of their strength and their ability to survive cancer while for others shame and embarrassment dominate their emotions.

Hair loss can be intensified by a variety of factors including hormone imbalances, genetics, stress, diet, and medical conditions such as diabetes, thyroid disorders, eating disorders, and autoimmune disorders like lupus or alopecia. Medicines for depression, heart disease, blood pressure, and inflammatory diseases can also contribute to hair loss.[5] And, of course, chemotherapy almost always causes hair loss. Just the threat of losing their hair causes some women to refuse or delay chemotherapy.

The FDA has approved only one medical treatment for female pattern hair loss (FPHL)—minoxidil or Rogaine—topically applied. Several drugs created and approved for other purposes, including antiandrogens, hormones, and others, are used "off label" but need to be closely monitored medically to assure safety.[6]

Other options include laser treatments and more natural approaches like nutritional supplements blended for this purpose, acupuncture, and shampoos with argan oil. Laser treatments may also decrease inflammation and simulate hair growth. Other old-fashioned notions could also help. These include developing stress management strategies as stress is a risk factor; avoiding hair dryers and tools that can damage and pull hair; massaging the scalp; and eating well, especially sufficient protein, iron, zinc, and vitamin B12. And, of course, wigs and extensions are popular responses to hair loss, with a global market expected to surpass $10 billion by 2023, growing nearly 10 percent each year.[7]

The hair replacement industry generally relies on human hair, with certain distinctions. In Remy hair extensions, all strands face the same way and often come from just one person's head. Virgin hair has not been processed. Double drawn refers to all hair being the same length. It can be attached with a weave—when strips of extra hair are sewn into thin plaits of the customer's own hair or attached to the customer's own hair using glue or micro rings. Extensions were initially popular with women in their 20s to 30s, but now the market includes many teenagers. Synthetic hair is less expensive but has limitations as it cannot be curled or straightened with heat.

The hair used for these replacements generally comes from countries where long, straight, dark hair is seen as beautiful but where the women are poor. Selling this valued asset is often the only way they can feed their families. This exploitation has forever been part of the industry and sometimes hair is even stolen—cut forcefully by a husband or a prison guard. Consumers and companies producing these increasingly desired products seem to ignore the karma involved. For example, Bianca Gascoigne, a British model and reality TV contestant, expressed, "I never ask where the hair comes from, I just love it so much. When you have big, bouncy hair you feel like a million dollars."[8]

"People always ask me how long it takes to do my hair.
I don't know, I'm never there."
—DOLLY PARTON[9]

A Public Face for a Private Problem

Ayanna Pressley was elected to the U.S. Congress from the Boston area in 2018. She was the first woman of color on the Boston City

Council and the first to represent Massachusetts in Congress. She had become used to the public eye through her competitive political campaigns, her work on the City Council and, before holding her own offices, as a staffer for high profile politicians like Joseph Kennedy II and John Kerry. Nothing could prepare her for the impact of losing her hair during her first term in Congress.[10]

One of the few African American women in Congress, Pressley wore her beautiful long hair in Sengalese twists much of the time—her signature look for the five years before she was elected. Some saw this as a political act but Pressley was proud of it and felt true to herself with this style; she frequently received letters thanking her for being a role model for girls and other women of color. About one year into her first term, her hair started to fall out. Pressley cared for it very intentionally but, bit by bit, it happened, and her last hair fell out right before a historic and momentous day: the Congressional vote for the first impeachment of the 45th president of the United States. It was a public day and Pressley stood up to it, but she wore a wig, not ready to bare her head. She has since been very transparent about her hair loss and what it has meant to her. She is still a strikingly beautiful woman, as her spirit and strength shine, with or without hair on her head.

Alopecia is the medical term for human hair loss. It is essentially an autoimmune disorder, with the body attacking itself and interfering with the normal process of hair growth and replacement. It can affect certain parts of the scalp, causing irregular bald spots (alopecia areata), or the whole scalp (totalis), or the whole body (universalis). Other subtypes are postpartum, androgenic (male pattern baldness—the most common), barbae (beard), cicatricial (under the skin) and traction (due to the persistent tightness of braids or other hairstyles).[11] Hair often grows back over time. In the meantime, Ayanna Pressley has been a model of personal agency, self-empowerment, and self-acceptance, demonstrating that appearance does not define us while being honest about what her hair has meant to her.

Pressley has partnered with the National Alopecia Areata Foundation (NAAF) and introduced federal legislation to amend Title XVIII of the Social Security Act, acknowledging wigs (also known as cranial prosthetics) as "durable medical equipment."[12] Ayanna

Pressley is doing something I love: walking her talk! Knowing first-hand that alopecia areata is a serious problem with far-reaching health consequences for many, she is advocating for these critical advances in both public awareness and medical coverage.

Hair Replacement

Of course, finding a hair stylist who can tune into your concerns and help you discover the best style to manage hair loss and all the feelings it brings can make this life issue far less traumatic and more manageable. Because these conditions often bring shame and embarrassment, alternatives to a more public retail experience are a welcome if infrequent option. Wigz on Wheelz in London is a service catering to people with alopecia, trichotillomania (hair pulling compulsion) and hair thinning and those undergoing gender reassignment. This mobile salon specializing in hair loss actually travels to people's homes or to hospitals in London and the home counties. Inspired by his mother and sister who were hairdressers and by the pain he saw when women lost their hair due to cancer treatment, founder Demitri Jones and his partner Marc Deacon have an important and inspiring mission.[13]

The wig world is a complex subculture and a pricy one. Synthetic wigs range from $5 to a few hundred dollars, while a natural wig ranges from $100 to $3,000.[14] Maintaining a wig's look and feel takes time and sometimes special tools or techniques, but this is easier today with help from the Internet. A bespoke wig or hairpiece is individually designed and custom made so can be more costly.

In the orthodox Jewish community, covering women's hair is considered a way to honor the intimacy of their marriages, so many will buy their first wig as part of the wedding preparation. Orthodox women may spend $1,500 for a basic style or up to $5,000 for a luxury, bespoke wig. The cost of monthly maintenance—washing, styling, maybe even some seasonal highlights—makes this a significant investment. This is a big business and a significant economic driver in women's personal spending.[15]

A new and exciting shopping option for wigs is a startup company now located in Boston led by three Gen Z women. Recent college grads Mary Imevbore, Tiiso McGinty, and Susana Hawken, classmates at Williams College, soon became entrepreneurs due to the gap in the marketplace for women of color looking for wigs. Mary had been searching for simple, quick, and easy ways to manage her natural hair, avoid chemical relaxers, and maintain a busy and demanding academic schedule. Wigs were a logical solution, but the resources were extremely limited, especially for young women of color. Concerned about this gap, the three friends researched options and new business models on the Internet and came up with an idea for their company Waeve. It offers six wig styles in either synthetic or human hair, reasonably priced from $72 to $398.[16]

Their first collection, "Days of the Week," is based on the notion that we have different needs at different times and our hair should be able to change easily. This inspiring trio of young women are onto something, including that the natural hair movement has created an additional segment of the wig and hair replacement market whose needs have not yet been fully met. A direct-to-consumer model has been successful for other products and may be particularly helpful to women who are struggling with their natural hair or who do not have time to invest in hair care but want to celebrate their hair with a different look.

According to projections by the French research firm Report-Linker, spending on wigs and hair extensions in North America may reach $2 billion by 2026.[17] Historically, the film and entertainment industries have been major markets for wigs and extensions. Increasing numbers of celebrities, models and other social media influencers wear them as well. While inspired by the unmet needs of black women, Waeve may fill a significant hole in the hair replacement marketplace.

The Girl with the Hair /
The Girl with the Hairpiece

Stephanie Dolgoff, a popular writer on women's issues and author of *My Formerly Hot Life: Dispatches from Just the Other Side of Young*,[18] shared her *hair story* with me. It speaks to how hair comes to define us and how hair loss can represent a significant loss of self.

> My whole life, they called me the Girl with the Hair—I had a mass of wild corkscrew ringlets that walked into a room moments before the rest of me did, and then lingered after I left. It was my "brand" in a way. As I got older, I became known for other, more important things, but that didn't make the blow to my sense of self any easier to bear when my hair started seriously thinning. I had always felt secure in my appearance, but all of a sudden, I needed reassurance about my hair, especially whether the thinning was obvious to others. It brought me back to freshman year in high school, when a boy asked me to pull my hair back away from my face and then announced that I was "nothing" without it. While I still had lots of hair, I moved from being preoccupied to being intermittently obsessed. I set out to find the cause of my hair loss and did everything I could to deal with it. Several doctors later, one of them said that no one looking at me would think I had a problem. I was still really worried, afraid that I might be forced to let go of being the Girl with the Hair. I loved that image, that part of my identity. Luckily, as time went on and I made some changes in my life to reduce my stress level, my hair rebounded. What a relief![19]

Despite Stephanie's track record of accomplishments and success, her thinning hair was unsettling and anxiety-provoking, but, lucky for her, that thick hair meant she had a lot to lose. Hair had always been a major contributor to her feeling attractive, so with its loss her self-confidence took a hit.

For women with thinner hair, the hair loss process is even more difficult. Irene is that woman whose hair was always thin and then midlife arrived, inevitably thinning it even more. Today's solutions to hair loss are complicated, so Irene has devoted immense amounts of time and energy to research and access the best answers for her.

In Irene's family, hair was very important. Her grandmother, mother and aunts would often say, "Your hair is your health and your wealth." Despite this very serious belief, the women in her family all have thin hair that they cover up in some way. Her grandmother's gray hair has been colored silvery blue for as long as Irene remembers. Although it is very thin, coloring and combing it just so camouflages this, and no one seems to notice. But as her mother approached midlife, her "health and her wealth" also began to disappear.

For decades now, Irene has worn a "rat," an oblong-shaped roll of hair, pinned in place with her own hair combed, sprayed, or teased over it. The "rat" gives volume and depth to sparse hair, but her mother also sprays a brown powder on her hair so the bald areas of her scalp do not show through. Worried for years about the health risks, Irene compulsively studied the medical literature and never found any evidence of toxicity so, when her hair inevitably began to thin, Irene too started using her mother's spray. Her worries about the safety of this spray never quite went away, so she stopped spraying and, at her mother's urging, got a hair transplant.

Always a good researcher and informed consumer, she went to one of the top doctors known for transplants in New York City. The process was painful, and her scalp never became comfortable after the surgery, so Irene gave up rather than pursuing more. Transplants are expensive, involving several procedures usually, at anywhere from $3,000 to $5,000 each. The pain—financial and physical— just was not worth it. Permanent weaves were not a great answer for Irene either. As your own natural hair keeps growing, to continue to look natural, the weave needs to be adjusted, requiring visits to the hair salon every two weeks. For a busy single parent in a demanding profession, this was beyond what she could commit to. Still, she searched for the solution to her dilemma.

The next step on Irene's journey was a hairpiece. She was excited initially by the prospect of solving her problem more permanently. And, in her typical thorough fashion, she has shopped all over the country and Internet to get the right replacement. Irene describes going from place to place trying to find the best hairpiece, sitting in showrooms and waiting rooms, visiting countless websites while feeling guilty, thinking that she was there "just for vanity while everyone else was there for cancer." Especially now as she gets older, Irene wants to improve her comfort with her appearance, so she wrestles with the inconvenient feelings and the many hassles involved with having a hairpiece.

After many tries, Irene finally did find a good quality piece that looks very natural and is dyed just the color of her own hair. It swings when she walks, looking vibrant and healthy, matching her warm and outgoing personality and ready smile. In fact, if I did not know her story, I would never have guessed that she wore a hairpiece. While

Irene loves its look and texture, hair pieces do move around, almost with a mind of their own, causing many unnerving moments. Irene loves to have her hair on when she swims in a lake or an ocean, but her hair has nearly floated away several times. Swimming at her local pool is also a challenge. She waits until no one is in the locker room, quickly puts her head in a locker, takes her hairpiece off and puts her swim cap on. She follows a similar routine after her swim. Time in the locker room must be added to her schedule, but the greatest challenge is acting casual and natural as others come and go around her and she stands fully clothed with her bathing cap on or keeps her head in the locker for an awkwardly long time. Irene wants no one to see her thin hair and bare scalp, so this is the price she must pay.

Since her divorce 12 years ago, Irene has been reluctant to date for this very reason. Getting ready for first dates or blind dates is almost like getting ready for a high school prom, as she has a friend over to help her with her hair, securing it to her head so those natural movements, like hugging, kissing, or cuddling, will not result in embarrassment. And then she describes the anxiety she experiences while going through security at airports. Once, on a trip to the South, Irene had to take the hairpiece off because the metal pin that keeps it attached kept activating the security sensor. When she told the TSA guard that it was a hairpiece, the woman responded, "Don't worry, honey, we all wear them." Irene instantly relaxed, but knows she is destined for more uncomfortable times in future airport security lines. Although she loves the outdoors and hikes and walks frequently, low branches or wind are both enemies, making her hairpiece less secure and causing her to be less spontaneous and far more self-conscious.

Irene's favorite hair memories are of her college days, before it began to thin, when she used beer cans to straighten it. To this day, she craves that look and feeling of long, straight hair. Despite all the time, energy, and money her hair has required, she still sees it as an essential component of the feelings she wants to have about herself as she ages—she wants "to be an old, bold woman who can project a natural self." As she says, "our relationship with our hair mirrors the aging process—it is symbolic of our relationship with ourselves as we age." Growing up in a family that stressed that hair "is your health and your wealth," that body part has played an enormous role in her psychological experience. Despite all those pressures, Irene has a great attitude toward life and has not let her thinning hair stop her, but all those trips to places like Nationwide Wigs have definitely affected her cash reserves.

"Hair was always my safe spot— until it wasn't"

Tina's story is a great example of the role hair plays in a woman's identity, self-esteem, and body confidence as well as the complex and unexpected feelings pregnancy can bring.

I first knew Tina when she had a very active eating disorder in her early 20s. She worked hard in therapy and had made tremendous progress on her symptoms. When we met again, she was at a new life stage—expecting her second child.

Tina's first child had been born when she was in her early 30s. An intelligent, psychologically astute, professional woman, she had not rushed into marriage and parenting. She felt prepared for this new life stage and had even anticipated some conflicting emotions as her pregnancy progressed. Tina had struggled with body image and weight issues since adolescence, but her hair had been her safety zone, giving her peace while the rest of her body evoked anxiety and often shame. During her pregnancy, the changes in her hair shocked her—this safe spot, her sanctuary, disappeared, disarming her and causing some depression during a time that many experience with jubilation.

When we met halfway through her second pregnancy, Tina was very focused on her mom-hair experience. She described how totally unprepared she had been for the changes in her hair during her first pregnancy. Because her appearance and weight had been such sources of anxiety, she had anticipated "feeling fat" and unattractive. However, she had never expected to lose so much hair. Tina's hair had always been her signature and she loved changing its color and making different statements with it. Knowing most women experienced hair loss post pregnancy, she felt especially cheated. During that first pregnancy, as her hair fell out, she felt increasingly adrift and unsure of herself.

Tina had made the decision to abstain from coloring her hair during her pregnancies, due to the potential risks to the fetus. She was worried enough about being a good mother and could not consider risking any possible harm to her baby. Losing the one body part that had always been a dependable source of self-esteem and confidence felt unfair to her.

The changes in Tina's hair represented many other issues but those were not as safe to discuss. Women often feel a mixture of complicated emotions when they are pregnant, but Western culture doesn't welcome any ambivalence—pregnant women are supposed to be happy, Madonna-like figures. Unprepared for what she would experience during this transformative time in her life, she felt far less free and that her life was now totally determined by her status as a mother. She wanted a healthy marriage but, having watched her parents divorce, she was not sure she had what it would take to maintain the commitment marriage requires. Having children brought up all these issues, and now even her hair felt uncertain. The changes on top of her head rattled her deep inside.

Tina's caution about hair color was warranted. Some medical resources suggest that women not treat their hair, especially in the first trimester, while others suggest that with careful following of directions to limit the time of exposure and fumes, chemical treatments and semi-permanent formulas can be safe.[20]

For many women, pregnancy is a time of great angst—worrying about the health of the baby, feeling so responsible should anything go wrong, and even feeling unsure about their ability to take care of this little one. Thus, they are reluctant to take a risk with hair color and start that progression into mom-hair early. They feel less attractive as their bodies change and less youthful if gray or mousy-looking hair creeps in, and this transition to motherhood has its costs. For Tina, the decisions about how to keep her hair color acceptable to her but safe for the baby were draining.

Hair thinning also shook Tina's sense of self. Hair loss affects 40 to 50 percent of pregnant women and is actually a normal variant of hormonal shifts.[21] For all of us, 10 percent of our hair follicles are in a resting stage at any point in time, but during pregnancy, this percentage can be higher. The increased hormonal activity keeps hair from falling out, but three to four months after birth, as the hormones calm down, hair will fall out and might feel significant to a woman for whom everything else is changing.

Tina's hair had thinned during her pregnancy, and she was experiencing all the dreaded changes in her body shape while her hair betrayed her as well. Somehow, she survived the pregnancy and the feelings about the loss of the body part that had always brought her pleasure and helped her feel attractive. Psychotherapy surrounding her body image and eating issues when she was younger had given her many resources that came in handy during this transition in her life.

Women who are ambivalent about the new stage in their life and all it brings may be especially troubled by hair loss and see it as just more sacrifice and loss of their identity. The good news is that the hair loss is temporary, although some women, like Tina, feel their hair is never quite the same.

Bald in the Land of Big Hair

At 32, recently transplanted to Houston with her husband and two young children, Joni Rodgers was suddenly diagnosed with lymphoma. What a difference a day makes. One day, life was checkered with the normal worries of a mother and wife, and the next day, Joni's bone marrow was being biopsied and a catheter port was surgically implanted. Losing her hair was right around the corner. Advised by her oncologist about alopecia, Joni kept saying things like "That's the least of my worries," but it turned out that her experience was not quite that simple. Her hair had far more meaning to her than she had realized and losing it was like losing a vital organ.[22]

Pre-cancer, Joni admits she was oblivious to the role her hair played in her sense of herself as a woman. As she puts it, "I was stunningly ungrateful for my hair. I always complained about mine and was jealous of everyone else's." Like so many adolescent girls whose waves or curls had a mind of their own, she spent painful, and very hot, hours ironing her hair. That was until that momentous first day of high school when, anxious about everything a girl anticipates as she steps out of childhood and into the future, the iron slipped, and she branded herself with a stripe right down the middle of her nose. Even that experience did not make her think much about what hair meant to her, but cancer surely did.

Her oncologist may have warned Joni about the inevitability of losing her hair soon after chemo started, and Joni may have felt ready for this. But alopecia is more than a bald head that can be covered with a scarf or baseball cap. It often starts with losing pubic hair—and not to a Brazilian bikini wax, today's odd fad. That naked, infant-like state brings up so many issues regarding femininity and sexuality, but losing eyelashes and eyebrows makes an even more profound statement. As Joni describes alopecia: "It is such a blatant, outward sign that something is wrong with your body. Everyone can see it. You don't look like normal people anymore. You feel so removed from normalcy and so removed from other people. So alone."

Joni tends to be a proactive, take-charge person, so when she began to lose her pubic hair and eyelashes, she started the ritual through which she would say goodbye to the long auburn tresses that she had taken for granted. She calls this her "You can't fire me—I quit" attitude and it serves her well. After a few days of brushing, braiding, stroking, and appreciating her hair for once, she asked a friend to help. They lifted her auburn hair from midway down her back and made 11 braids, then her friend cut them off, leaving half an inch of hair all over her head. She carefully wrapped the braids and stored them in a drawer. Joni thought this gradual change in her appearance would soften the blow for her children. Of course, within days, that half-inch stubble started to fall out, ushering in a new stage for all of them. Soon, to show his support and solidarity, her husband shaved his head.

Joni's hair remained a powerful force connecting the family throughout her treatment. Her will to recover was motivated by her love for her children and her desire to protect them from any pain, but her children were just as eager to help her. Carefully, her seven-year-old son would get the braids out of the drawer where she kept them and hold them up to her head. Joni would share the curls she had saved from his first haircut to show him that he could look different but still be the same person and reassure him that she was still the same mom she always had been. The remnants of their shorn hair connected and comforted them. During this time, he learned to make dream catchers, and he soon made a healing mandala with her braids, symbolizing her resilience by showing the resilience of her hair.

Joni had so many poignant, gut-wrenching moments stimulated by her hair loss. At the gym one day, trying desperately to do something that would feel normal, Joni recalls bending over the water fountain for a drink. When she stood up, the man waiting for a drink saw that this bald head belonged to a woman. He instantly crossed the gym to drink from a different fountain. Even if she had wanted to deny her illness, everyone else could see that something was terribly wrong with Joni.

Despite all the pain and loneliness her hair loss brought, Joni saw her profound sense of isolation as one of the gifts that cancer can bring. Her hair loss forced her to face herself in a way that continuing her normal life would never have required. And she has been facing herself ever since.

For years after her chemotherapy, Joni kept her hair in a buzz-cut. She was afraid of becoming attached to her hair again. But she was also reluctant to let go of what she calls her hermitage—the calm peace of separation from normal life brought on by her cancer. The isolation of her illness gave her time to write her first novel, a dream she had since childhood, and launched her into a career of writing and publishing. She was unsure how having hair again would affect her journey as an artist, but, after eight years of a post-chemotherapy buzz-cut, her daughter challenged her to go for a year without cutting her hair. Again, her children's reaction to her hair and its meaning pushed Joni forward in her personal development and in her recovery. Her son, at the age of seven, helped her make peace with her bald head, and, eight years later, her daughter helped her to embrace life with hair again. Joni found that she could have long hair and still dedicate herself to the creative and introspective process of writing. Now she celebrates herself through her life as an artist and through her long hair, with blond instead of auburn covering the gray. As with so many women, what happens on top of her head is a mirror for what is happening inside her head and heart—today she is alive and well, vibrant and engaged, and so is her hair.

About a decade after her cancer treatment, Joni published her book *Bald in the Land of Big Hair*,[23] reminding readers that for a woman living in Texas, the land of the bouffant, losing her hair is the ultimate insult. Her book is about life, not about illness. It is about resilience, love, blind faith, and never giving up. It is a great read—deeply moving and funny at the same time. I strongly recommend it.

"You're so lucky"

For years, Paula constantly heard things like "You're so lucky. You can do anything with your hair." She explains that this was essentially true:

> With very little time and even less chemicals, I could achieve straight, wavy, or curly locks and everything in between. But I never imagined hair loss would fall in this wide spectrum of versatility. If anything, I would have embraced a little less hair…. If you asked me, my hair was a nuisance…. Let's just say the magnitude of my frizz was more reliable than the Weather Channel in the prediction of any climactic event involving moisture.

When I met Paula, she was 16 and in treatment for anorexia nervosa. In other words, her luck, and her hair, had begun to run out. When women suffer from eating disorders, their hair gradually thins due to malnutrition. The body simply cannot spare the protein needed for hair growth: it is using every nutrient it can access to stay alive. Paula's eating disorder had changed everything, including her hairline, but despite how hard her parents, family, physician and therapists repeatedly tried to get her to see how compromised her life and health had become, Paula was oblivious. No one got through to her, no matter how kind and loving, or how clinical and direct, the message was.

Finally, one day, sitting by herself in the den, looking at old family pictures, forced her to recognize the real impact of her starvation. In an "aha" moment, Paula recognized that what had once been a head of hair to be reckoned with had turned into a sad scalp with bald spots. For the first time, she cried long and hard. Her hair loss allowed her to see all the other losses she was suffering. Now she could no longer ignore the clumps of hair she would find every time she showered or brushed her hair. Paula needed a concrete sign of the damage she was doing to her body and her hair provided it. She was able to admit that her eating disorder sentenced her to a robotic existence and took all the pleasures, including that uncontrollable head of thick hair, away. Since then, her desire for recovery has become stronger and her hair has become the symbol of her progress. As she says, "The renewal of each strand forces the eating disorder further and further aside."

Paula was not all better when I last spoke with her, but her spirit and her hair are both more present. Her hair told her what she needed to do, and she listened. For so many women with eating disorders, "hitting bottom" happens when their hair loss hits them, enabling them to realize that they will be sentenced to a lifeless life unless they make major changes and begin to commit to recovery.

Sometimes, in fact, hair is the only motivator for recovery. One recovered woman, with very beautiful, thick hair and a spirit as strong as they come, told me, "Quite simply, vanity was the trigger for my recovery." Having met her, I am grateful for her vanity: she is making a difference in this world. Hair is a powerful messenger, capable of transforming us when other, more logical appeals cannot penetrate our defenses.

CHAPTER 11

What's Age Got to Do with It?

"There's a reason why 40, 50 and 60 don't look the way they used to, and it's not because of feminism, or better living through exercise. It's because of hair dye."—Nora Ephron[1]

Hair is the ultimate barometer for women's feelings about the aging process and the challenges we meet in each life stage. We may not be able to control other aspects of growing older, but we can do a lot to control our hair to deliver the image we want. This starts early in development, as preschool girls chop their hair when no one is watching to express identity and individuation issues, and continues right through mid-childhood, adolescence, early adulthood, midlife and beyond. As we navigate these developmental life transitions, hair tells important stories about us. This is especially true as we approach midlife and later, when both hair color and length become such hot issues.

The Feminist Chop or Liberating Length?

An article in the *New York Times* titled "Why Can't Middle-Aged Women Have Long Hair?" generated a record 1250 responses in one week, demonstrating just how hot the topic of hair length and age is.[2] Despite the criticism and commentary that her long hair evoked, Dominique Browning wrote that to her it is a sign of liberation from the stereotypes limiting women's experience: "My long hair is indeed a declaration of independence. I am rebelling, variously, against Procter & Gamble, my mother, Condé Nast and, undoubtedly, corporate America in general. Whereas it used to be short hair that was a hallmark of being a liberated woman … these days, long hair is a mark of liberation."

She elaborated that important people in her life all disapproved of her long hair—worrying about the ramifications for her professional credibility or that she was hiding behind it. Still, she felt good about it: "But in the middle of my life, I'm happy with it. Which is saying a lot about anything happening to my 55-year-old body…."

I remember where, when, and with whom I had the first discussion of how much longer we could have long hair. The three of us were in our middle to late 30s, highly educated, independent, and already accomplished in our careers. We all had rejected most of the traditional, gender-bound cultural roles but we still felt pressure to follow the rules about hair! While none of us cut our hair after that discussion, we were convinced that the clock was ticking on our long hair, just like the biological clock for decisions about children. These attitudes say a lot about how our culture treats women, causing us to spend endless energy on hair care, usurping our precious time and resources.

Gray Hair: The Gift of Life

Truth be told, gray hair is just a natural phenomenon that comes to those of us who are lucky enough to be alive through middle age. We should really see it as a gift of life! After we turn 30 or so, our hair follicles begin to produce hydrogen peroxide, which in turn blocks its ability to make melanin. With less melanin produced, our hair cannot retain its natural color, whatever that once was.[3]

Like other aspects of our bodies that we battle today, the "problem" of hair color is culturally constructed. Hair loss and changes in pigmentation of our hair are simply genetically programmed. Pigment cells, or melanocytes, within the hair's cortex, or middle layer, create hair color. As we move through the decades, these cells will inevitably be damaged or die, stripping color from the hair, creating the look of silver or white. While the most common cause of gray hair is genetic, stress can also contribute by depleting the body's stores of vitamin B. As a result, a third of women discover their first silver strand by the age of 30 and, by 50, the average woman has lost 50 percent of her original color.[4] Turning gray is not a personal failure or a character flaw. It is simply a fact of life, happening on its own accord.

Genetics drive the rate and pace of this transition. In other words, the changing nature of our hair color is an innate event—not a true sign of our self-worth or our productivity and value to the workplace, as cultural attitudes sometimes convey. Yet, hair dye formulas have been part of our history for at least 6,000 years—long a part of human civilization. During the Roman Empire, when hair naturally faded to gray, many efforts were made to counter this; ashes, walnut shells, worms, and other natural substances were used to create dyes. Both men and women used combs made of lead to darken their hair; they knew nothing of its impact on cognitive development like we do now.[5] Hair and its color has always had meaning.

"It is called premature graying—is graying
ever not premature to its victims?"
SUSAN BROWNMILLER[6]

So What's the Deal About Gray Hair?

The baby boomer generation, the "me generation," has consistently demanded to be taken seriously and espoused being "real"—except when it involves the natural evolution of their hair. Boomers, myself included, thrive on being accepted for who we really are, having worked hard to separate ourselves from our parents' generation. But this being "real" stops when it comes to hair color. It is as if we want to be remembered for the "real" look we had decades earlier, when we were 20 or 30 instead of 50, 60, 70 or more.

Rose Weitz, author of *Rapunzel's Daughters: What Women's Hair Tells Us About Women's Lives*,[7] suggests that women somehow have come to believe that we lose our "real self" if we do not insist on coloring our hair to match the color of our youth. Being more fake, more artificially constructed, somehow makes us more real, more genuine. How could that be? It only makes sense in a culture that needs women to not be fully empowered and in an economy that profits enormously from women's insecurities about their bodies and appearance.

Interestingly, because color photography was not widely available till the 1960s, we do not have a reliable historical record of hair color. Black and white photos simply do not tell the story. In the cinema, hair coloring was commonplace—black, red, or blond, but nothing more. Gray hair was reserved for grandmothers or other marginalized characters.

The advancement of advertising, mass media and consumer culture in the 20th century was a game-changer. In the 1950s and 1960s, after the Second World War, the United States and other Western nations were enjoying increased wealth and technological advancement. Time and money were available for more than just subsistence and survival, so consumer culture found ways for us to feel less satisfied and less content and to need more things to make us happy. Hair color was one of many new products that quickly became negotiable parts of women's lives. Natural hair color soon faded into a distant memory. Success and beauty for women would soon become associated with hair color, accounting for 17 percent of the hair and nail salon industry's revenue.[8]

Before the Clairol "Does she or doesn't she?" campaign, only about 7 percent of women dyed their hair. In less than 50 years, that increased to 60 percent. Clairol launched its do-it-yourself, 20-minute color treatment in 1956, with aggressive marketing campaigns associating gray hair with being unpopular, socially inferior, and basically a loser to be pitied. Yes—all because of hair color![9] In 2021, market research indicated that 75 percent of women colored their hair, with projections that this will continue to increase with an annual compounded growth rate of nearly 9 percent.[10] Nearly 70 percent of women report that having their hair colored makes them feel instantly more attractive.[11] Feeling attractive—that seductive magnet—brings women right back month after month to a habit that can end up costing them a small fortune over the decades.

On top of the pervasive impact of the 20th-century consumer culture, the 21st century in the United States ushered in a phenomenon called the anti-aging movement. This new trend in lifestyle and biomedical messaging soon became a $100–$300 billion industry with goals to eliminate or reverse aging, or at least to reduce its impact.[12] Prolonging life, or "life extension," as some call it, is a major component as are techniques to counter the evidence of aging through hormone treatments, cosmeceuticals, and cosmetic surgery.

According to Abigail Brooks, an expert in gender, aging and the sociology of the body,[13] for women, "aging well" means they must be constantly fighting the natural aging process, refusing to give into things like gray hair. She and many other feminists see the anti-aging industry as a bully, turning women against their bodies rather than allowing them to embrace and enhance the aging process.[14]

Appearance is key to the anti-aging images, and, once more, hair is a primary element of any visual impression. When we describe someone to a stranger, we tend to mention three things: height, shape (weight and/or frame) and hair color, painting a picture of this old or new friend. In an anti-aging culture, gray hair is instantly noticed—a target, especially for women.

"You know what's anti-aging? Death. Let's be happy we're aging."
CAROL WALKER[15]

The Gray Zone

Contemporary culture has historically given little respect to older women and going gray is a definite sign of age. Young women may be able to dye their hair gray for the fun of it, but once a woman has wrinkles along with the gray hair, her credibility plummets. Think about how few prominent American women wore their natural hair color prior to the pandemic. The fusion of fear of aging with economic well-being pulled so many into the endless web of hair color.

Age discrimination is a serious issue affecting women's earning power, maximizing the likelihood that a woman will consider covering her gray. Women's employment opportunities shrink as they age, compared to the opportunities available to their male peers or younger females. Women over the age of 50 are less likely to get a callback when applying for administrative support or secretarial roles. A report by the Federal Reserve Bank of St. Louis found that older women suffered the greatest impact on long-term unemployment rates after the 2007 U.S. recession. This economic crisis hit female workers 50 and older much harder than any other age group—male or female.[16]

More recently, the COVID-19 pandemic has also affected women more adversely than men. The industries they work in are more sensitive to the pandemic, causing many women to lose their jobs. And with schools, day care centers and other child-oriented services shut down or limited, women have had to take on those responsibilities as well. Fewer women work in jobs that permit telecommuting, further impacting women economically. The ramifications for women's employment and economic recovery will echo for years, maybe for generations.

An AARP study indicates that 72 percent of women between the ages of 45 and 74 believe that people face age discrimination at work, but only 57 percent of men believed this.[17] Since gender already affects income significantly, it is hard for women to ignore the impact gray hair might have on their earning power and their future retirement earnings. Economic inequities may unconsciously trap many women into covering up their natural color.

The Ultimate Catch-22

Hair color is the ultimate Catch-22 for feminists. The women's movement challenged so many of the limitations in women's lives, opening door after door—education, sports, career, economic freedom, sexuality, and birth control, just to name a few. Yet, at the same time, the choices regarding appearance became increasingly narrow, especially with our hair color. Ironically, feminism expanded

110

women's opportunities beyond what most imagined, but it contracted our acceptance of the aging process—our hair needs to look young. Best-selling novelist and journalist Elizabeth Benedict shamefully admits to membership in this cult "whose core belief—whose only belief—is that our fake hair color is essential to our well-being."[18] Yet even she could not escape, simply to avoid admitting her age.

Unlike our grandmothers, and even our mothers or older sisters, we can be astronauts, physicists, Olympians, billionaires, business leaders, symphony conductors, construction workers, attorneys, Supreme Court justices, surgeons, weightlifters, boxers, governors, and senators. Still, having natural—that would be gray—hair today may cast a midlife woman as the outsider. Instantly, others may think she must be a new age spirit or an old hippie or some other radical person. Many women are fearful that if they allow their gray hair to show, they will be considered less vital and less valuable in the workplace.

Race and culture also affect decisions about hair color. Non-white women living in Western countries know that kinky natural hair has too often been seen as unattractive and unacceptable. Adding gray hair to that picture may feel way too risky and disempowering, leading many to color their hair to offset the impact of the natural kink. And for Latina women, dark hair can be an important connection to their ethnic identity. Coloring it is a politically active step, promoting their Latin heritage.[19]

For women returning to work after time off to raise their children or for other family responsibilities, having a modern hairstyle with no gray showing also seems required. While healthcare, non-profits, and academia may tolerate a more natural look, business, sales, law, politics, marketing, public relations, and many other professions are not friendly environments to women as they age.

What's Your Color?

Consciously or not, most women grapple with this issue and, like me, most adult women cannot tell you their true hair color. Just as we may be curious about someone's astrological sign, we might also want to know her natural hair color.

Many of the women I interviewed struggle with not being completely natural. As one woman explained her decision, "My hair is gray now—it started in my early 50s. For me, coloring it is just about vanity—I don't look good with gray hair. Oddly enough, I would never have plastic surgery, but I will color my hair. I just want to strike a blow for older women looking good." Another woman who is in her early 60s reflects similar sentiments: "My life is an open book when it comes to my hair—I don't try to hide anything except its color. I actually don't want to color my hair, but I looked prematurely old. It's definitely a little dystonic to color my hair—I'm a nature girl, outside a lot. I really don't fuss with clothes. I dress casually and don't wear makeup. In fact, my hair is my biggest personal expense."

A woman I love and respect deeply, approaching 80 at the time, said to me over lunch one day: "My husband's salt and pepper hair distinguished him; mine aged me 10 years. So I started coloring my hair and I never stopped—and I won't."

To add to the confusion, gray hair occasionally appears on young women on fashion runways. Modeling icons like Victoria Beckham and Kate Moss have opted for the look of granite from time to time as has Lady Gaga.

The last time gray hair was really in fashion was the 18th century. Then, both sexes worked hard to achieve that gray look, using powder covered by oil so it would not rub off. In fact, the wig powder used by the French aristocracy was a ground starch that had become a tight commodity during the Flour War of 1775. When flour prices were deregulated, the lower classes could not afford bread, while the upper class used this precious commodity to whiten their hair. The poor may have been starving, but wealthy heads were well starched until the end of the French Revolution. Marie Antoinette was known for her huge white bouffant hairdos, but legend has it that her hair actually turned gray the night before her beheading. Soon, hair powder would be taxed, and gray hair was no longer desired.[20] Hair always tells a story.

From "Does she or doesn't she?" to "Will she or won't she?"

During the 2020 pandemic, when hair salons and other personal services were not available due to the rapid spread of the virus in close quarters, many women struggled with what to do about the obvious gray taking over their heads. Some allowed their natural hair color to show and others did what they could with boxes of hair dye and coaching from a friend or stylist, often in their driveway or a cold garage. And, of course, a few broke the rules and went into salons against public policy, feeling desperate to see a familiar head in the mirror since our world had become so unfamiliar, with facemasks and social distancing limiting our social contacts.

The decision to cover the gray or go natural became a major dilemma for countless women. At the same time, a new movement was growing: a conscious and intentional embrace of gray hair. On both Facebook and Instagram, a "silver sisterhood" has sprung up, with women sharing stories and advice about the experience of going gray. These positive and lively exchanges promise to ease women into this new life stage if they choose it.[21]

There have always been some countervailing voices to cultural trends: brave and independent souls who listen to their gut instincts and act on their truth. Once she realized that she had spent $65,000 on masking her gray hair in only 20 years, Anne Kreamer, author of *Going Gray*,[22] decided to give up the war with her natural color. As it is for most women, coloring her hair was initially intended to make her appear relevant and vibrant as she aged. In fact, disguising your age does the opposite, as it makes you less real and less genuine. At 47, Kreamer was almost always the only woman in a room with natural color, and even 20 years later, she found the same panorama as she looked around a room. Her decision to go gray allowed her to evolve and move forward. She sees how hard she was trying to avoid "growing up" by covering the gray.

To Kreamer, decisions about hair color are like a personal flag, making "to dye or not to dye" an important question for each of us. If women were more honest and more transparent, telling our individual truths instead of hiding and covering up, maybe our culture could do the same. Decisions about our hair reflect our reactions to our culture and our society and we need to make them consciously and intentionally—and to own them.

By the way, Kreamer expected that a gray head would impact dating more than work. Her research found the opposite—men were very attracted to her natural look but potential employers' doors slammed in her face. She even proposed a Gray Hair Equal Opportunity Act to protect us against haircolorism in the workplace.

Gray Is the New Blonde

And now there is a new movement afoot or ahead! In 2013, actress, producer and director Victoria Marie released a YouTube video of her hair journey called "Gray Is the New Blonde."[23] When she moved to Los Angeles to pursue acting a few years later, she was shocked at the hostility the entertainment industry expressed toward women with gray hair. Remembering the tremendous excitement her earlier YouTube video had generated, Victoria decided to pour her energy into a documentary film with a mission "to show the world how beautiful natural, gray hair can be and to provide encouragement for all those seeking it. And in the process move towards acceptance and eventual reverence as enjoyed by our male counterparts."

Victoria has been living her own hair story. As she says, "People have been talking to me about my hair from day one!" She was born with jet black hair—and so much of it—that the nurses put a ribbon in it the day she was born! Perhaps it was pure destiny that, decades later, she would be a champion for women to accept their natural beauty and their natural hair.[24]

Victoria's hair had gone gray nearly overnight after 9/11. She had been living in New York City and had just started a new business when she experienced the trauma of that day and its aftermath. Within weeks, she packed up and returned to her home state of North Carolina. She had short hair at the time and was always using color, but before she realized it, the roots started to show. Suddenly, her hair "didn't count" as it had for so long and her energy had been focused on emotional recovery and moving forward after experiencing the unparalleled trauma of 9/11. In 2012, pursuing an acting career, she colored her hair once more, anticipating she would get more work opportunities, "but it didn't feel like me." Life has taught her that "the most important thing is to be true to yourself and hair is one way to do that."

Now Victoria's message empowers other women to be true to themselves. As we age, we can become more ourselves, pursuing our values and interests. In reality, how women feel about themselves is more important than hair color or any other aspect of appearance. She asserts that gray hair does not define a woman, especially if she is "full of life, vim and vigor, following her passions."

Western women are systematically conditioned to believe that gray hair will make a woman look tired and old and "done." In the process of going gray, however, many will let go of the fears about fitting in and the pressures they have felt to be quiet and unobtrusive. Countless women find themselves as they make this transition, but Victoria is quick to say that gray hair is not for everyone, and no woman should feel "put down or less than" if she doesn't go gray or if she tries it and then returns to coloring her hair.

Once they stopped coloring their hair, many of the women cast in *Gray Is the New Blonde* experienced feeling free for the first time, empowered as they never had been before. Women grow up using all kinds of hair products from a young age, most of which we know little about. For some, the awareness that they were no longer putting potentially toxic chemicals on their scalps every few weeks was liberating. For those who face cancer or other health issues affecting their hair, getting rid of hair color chemicals can be a life-affirming step toward reclaiming their health.

The "right to choose"

Stimulated by the provocative issues raised by Victoria Marie in this video, we appear to be moving toward a time when women will feel freer to make decisions about hair care and appearance based on their best interests and their own desires. The question for women may change from "Does she or doesn't she?" to "Will she or won't she?"

Prompted by the impact of the COVID pandemic on access to hair care services as well as the existential questions we have been facing, countless social media sites have emerged preaching the notion of color-free hair care. Hashtags include names like #GrayHairDontCare, #SilverSisters ,#Grayhairrevolution, and #Grombre (gray meets ombré) that espouses a "radical celebration of the natural phenomenon of gray hair," with hundreds of thousands of followers and smiling faces.

For many, especially those with financial resources, the path to natural hair color will include a well-paid stylist who can advise them how to go through this transition comfortably. Jack Martin is a high-profile colorist to the stars with clients including Jane Fonda, Andie McDowell, and Sharon Osbourne and has more than 640,000 followers on Instagram. (See jackmartincolorist.)

His talent is finding a chemical version of a woman's natural color, as there are many shades of gray and silver, including blue silver, white silver, silver silver, charcoal silver, even lavender silver. He discovers their natural color by stripping the color from their treated hair, leaving the natural roots which is now the prototype for their new color. The roots will match the newly growing treated hair. This process takes 10 hours when done in one sitting. In time their natural color will cover their whole head and no longer need any help to achieve that. Some choose a slightly different tint or tone— more silver, perhaps—so they may need some color a few times a year but not every month. Good colorists can work themselves out of a job.[25]

Accepting her natural hair color can be one of the most empowering steps a woman can take as she ages. Does she continue to follow the crowd and drink the cultural Kool-Aid that disempowers women and diminishes their natural beauty? Does she become "beauty sick," acquiescing to cultural pressures related to appearance and spending more time facing the mirror than facing the world?[26] Or doesn't she? Will she make her own decisions and draw her own lines in her life? Or won't she? This is a time for women to take back the power in their lives—starting with their hair color. The "right to choose" includes hair color, and any choice a woman consciously makes will empower her.

CHAPTER 12

Tangles, Snarls and Transitions

"The truth is that hair transitions are personal transitions, expressions of a deeper tumult—rough edges and breaking waves."—Diane Simon[1]

Hair tells a story, especially when it comes to a woman's attempts to disentangle herself from relationships and realities that limit her or just no longer fit. For most women, a storyboard with headshots is all she would need to tell her entire life story—both what was happening inside her heart and what her life looked like to others. Women routinely pursue a new "hair do" to "un-do" a major problem in their lives. Just think about how many women use a new hairstyle or color to punctuate the ending of a relationship and a new beginning more based on their own desire for independence and recognition.

First Lady Michelle Obama turned 49 just days before her husband was inaugurated for the second time. She explained a decision about her hair as an emotional one: "This is my mid-life crisis, the bangs. I couldn't get a sportscar. They won't let me bungee jump so instead I cut my bangs."[2] She needed some symbolic change in her life and could not make bigger ones due to the unusual position of being the nation's First Lady. She stirred a national conversation but not about midlife crises—really just about bangs. In no time, her bangs had a Twitter handle providing humor but, with all due respect to the Twitter account, no insight into the meaning of bangs. Whether the bangs truly represented a midlife crisis, we do not know, but the First Lady needed to do something new and that was the best she could manage.

In her one-woman play *How to Draw a Nekkid Man*, artist Tricia

Rose Burt describes a critical period of transition in her life.[3] She realized she was "following the shoulds" instead of living an authentic life. Eschewing the good girl, she divorces her husband, gives up her business career, moves to another country, and later relocates in New England. Once a traditional Southern belle and businesswoman, she moved into a career in the arts, initially visual and then performance, refining her natural talent in storytelling.

During this challenging and unsettling time, one particularly transformative bit of advice from a wise friend was "You should dye your hair—might make you feel a little perky." She chose red, a color she had secretly desired for a long time. Based on what I know about her career and life, she has been perky ever since. Decades later, she still wears this color and sees it as an empowering step enabling her to live the life she wants, less directed by others. Recently adding to her video performances, she produced a short how-to video, "How to Dye Your Hair at Home (During a Global Pandemic),"[4] full of useful and humorous advice about "how to shelter in place looking like a million dollars." For $9 a month, a box of Nice'n Easy natural dark auburn color has continued to be her mainstay during this global crisis. This hair color feels so natural to her, and no one even guesses that it isn't: it is like she corrected Mother Nature, landing on her true and authentic self—inside and out.[5]

Tricia Rose Burt is not the only one to use her hair to punctuate a new life stage. After divorcing her unfaithful husband, the well-known surrealist artist Frida Kahlo painted herself in a man's suit with her long black hair shorn on the ground around her. She cut her hair each time she learned of her husband's affairs. In the painting's background she wrote: "Look, if I loved you, it was because of your hair. Now that you are without hair, I don't love you anymore," the words of a Mexican song.[6]

Using hair to get rid of a man's influence is familiar territory. The song "I'm Going to Wash That Man Right Outta My Hair" from the musical *South Pacific* has become a worldwide favorite, recorded by countless artists over the years,[7] although it may take more than shampoo to move forward.

Sometimes, hair has been part of the problem in a relationship, a battleground with a controlling spouse. Women generally feel

pressure from men to wear their hair long, whether they themselves like the look (and the work) or not. One husband listed his wife's refusal to change her hair color and length as one of the reasons he divorced her. She vows to never compromise herself in relationships and wears her hair like her trademark.

"Coming out"

Hair often plays a central role in moments of the "coming out" process for LGBTQI individuals. Again, since it is so visible, so symbolic, and so easily changed, hair readily conveys a message about gender and sexual identity. According to market research by Procter & Gamble, 60 percent of LGBTQI individuals change their hair when they are transitioning or making major life changes. It could be chopping hair off, growing it long, or using a wig or hair piece to get more hair on their heads. It could be to look more masculine, more feminine, or neither—a non-binary image instead. Informed by this data, P&G has formed a partnership between their Pantene product line and the Gay and Lesbian Alliance Against Defamation (GLAAD). Their Power to Transform campaign is designed to help communities challenge gender stereotypes and bias and overcome resistance, negativity, and inertia.[8] The visual transformation, be it subtle and same, or dramatic and gender-bending, can punctuate the internal process—possibly the safest first step for a coming out process or affirmation of a new gender identity.

The pressures gay women feel about their sexual preferences often translate into attention to hair. Sensing that their environment is not accepting or safe, some choose an overly feminine appearance to offset their sexuality. Kerry, a gay woman in her 20s, had worn her Farrah Fawcett–like beautiful and bountiful blond hair long throughout her teens and early adulthood to keep her family of origin happy. As she said: "Everyone loved my hair. They talked about it a lot. It was really a constant conversation. In a way, it was how I felt loved and appreciated. Now I realize the love was conditional and I never really felt safe or secure."

Although her family knew she was a lesbian, this head of hair provided enough cover that they could overlook that truth. Kerry, however, desperately wanted the inside and the outside to be in sync. More and more each day, she felt like a fake, an "imposter," not the daughter her parents wanted her to be nor who she wanted to be. No surprise, when she came home with her hair cut chin-length, her parents expressed deep grief and disappointment—and even shock. They had appeared able to accept her choices until she took this step. Cutting her hair was an act of independence and defiance that they could not ignore.

Kerry realized that her unusually beautiful head of hair had made her easy to love in this rigid, conservative family, but she did not want her closest relationships to be so conditional. This public, external message about her sexual orientation caused a significant disconnection in her family and it has lasted years. Although Kerry had anticipated her decision would upset the equilibrium in her family, she desperately needed to be true to herself. Since then, she has created many new relationships—her "chosen family"—and feels that she is living a more honest and truly loving life. She thanks her hair for that gift.

Beyond Butch and Femme: Today's Gay Woman's Hair Story

The LGBTQI hair story goes far beyond the old dichotomous descriptors of the past. "Butch" or "femme" is now butch, femme, sporty, professional, soft butch, androgynous or just plain cool when it comes to hair choices.

What was a fairly predictable set of choices not long ago is much more complicated now. The women's movement unleashed so many educational, career and political opportunities, making all women's lives much more complex. Hair choices have evolved right alongside them. This is a complicated subject for many in the LGBTQI community, as Jennifer describes:

As I began to write about my personal gay hair story, I became even more baffled by the question: is who I am how I wear my hair or is how I wear my hair who I am? I began to realize that as far as we have come in today's modern society in accepting homosexuality, and as out as I think I am and have been, I have been hiding behind my hair!

I hide because of how I choose to wear my hair, and my hair protects me. The hard truth is that my hair makes it easy for me to "pass" as a straight woman! I would like to think that is not one of the reasons why I have chosen to wear my hair this way, but I must be honest with myself.... My hair in its natural state is a bit like what I perceive the real me to be most of the time, the gay me. It is frizzy, unruly, and sometimes out of control.

My hair after I am done with it is anything but. My hair after I have molded the hair story I am trying to tell, and after the product I apply, the time it takes to blow dry and the use of the "straightening iron" PUN INTENDED—to make it what it is not naturally—tamed, straight, flowing, feminine, and professional, tells my workplace, my gay sisters, and strangers a totally different story. It tells them that I am feminine, soft, and straight, when really, I am butch, hard and gay!

Despite the progress we have made in accepting the complexity of all women's lives today and acknowledging the challenges the LGBTQI individuals face, Jennifer's heartfelt comments show that we are only partway there. Contemporary culture continues to be suspicious of differences and more comfortable with the past and more traditional ways of looking at gender—and at hair.

"Since you can't actually jump out of your skin"

Hair can be a safety valve, the only pressure reliever available, so cutting, coloring, or changing it in some other dramatic way sometimes feels like the only option as one woman described:

At one point in my life, I was having a phase of horrible anxiety attacks. I almost cut all of my hair off, myself, with my sewing shears. It was after Britney Spears had had her rather public breakdown where she shaved her head, and I remember thinking that I could totally understand why she did that. Since you can't actually jump out of your skin, cutting off all my hair seemed like the next best thing to get rid of that feeling. But I didn't. I breathed through it. It took almost a whole weekend, but the urge passed. I'm OK and my hair is too.

Hairstyle changes—even dramatic ones like shaving her head or doing a drastic color job—feels so much safer than lots of other potential steps a woman might take to define a new time in her life. After all, hair will grow back or grow out or can be restyled, even if it takes a lot of time, effort and money. It is less traumatic than leaving a relationship or a job, moving, or other major transformative decisions. And it is far less permanent than other things she might do to her body, like getting plastic surgery, tattoos or piercings that also make visible public statements. A baseball cap, a scarf or even a wig can cover up anything that goes wrong with a new hairstyle.

"My mid-life crisis happened right on top of my head"

As soon as we sat down to talk about her hair, Joan said, "My mid-life crisis happened right on top of my head." She eagerly described the importance hair has had throughout her life.

> From the time I was a little girl, I knew hair had power. I had these pretty ringlets, and everyone wanted to touch my hair. My mom really loved it so when I was a teenager, I cut it off, just to spite her. She cried like a baby. A few years later, my older sister developed cancer and the worst day was when a piece of her hair fell in the sink. It made it real. I did everything I could to help—bought her great turbans—but the hair loss had a profound impact on me. It has continued to be the medium I use to express myself. So when I turned 40, and was feeling a lot of negative things about getting older, I took the heat off some of those other issues by going blond. I always wanted to, but it was very weird—I didn't feel like myself and it almost seemed like my husband was cheating on me with this blond!
>
> I remember having lunch with a friend, telling her that everyone seems to like my hair and she said, "They are just saying that because they don't love you enough to tell you the truth. It looks horrible." The next day I went back to the hairdresser. Then I had red hair for a month.

Hair had been a way to individuate and to disconnect from her mother during Joan's adolescence. Later, her sister's hair loss due to cancer treatment made Joan keenly aware of the importance of many things including their connection, the fragility of our health, and the aging process. Turning 40 and entering a new life stage were disorganizing to Joan. She was afraid of getting old and changing her hair allowed her to feel in control of life again. A close friend's honest response to her metamorphosis caused her to rethink her hair decisions. A month as a redhead went by fast but was not what she was looking for, so she stopped making dramatic changes. Now she sees her hair as a way "to have fun on the top of my head" and she has gradually worked out the many issues that were underlying that blond decision.

"Hair matters in our culture because it is a way, perhaps the most important way, women transform themselves."
—GRANT MCCRACKEN[9]

The Long and the Short of It

Many a *hair story* shows how a "new 'do" represents a desire for a "new me" or for some way to disentangle from the snarls of life and to transition forward. Hair alone can't do this as Joan's story tells us, but hair can symbolize a commitment to a renewed and healthier approach to life's issues.

Hair length is associated with many powerful stories. The long hair on the heads of all fairy tale figures, goddesses, and female Disney characters is not likely just a simple coincidence. Rapunzel's flowing blond hair was her escape from spinsterhood and isolation. In the Old Testament, when Delilah ordered a servant to cut his hair, Samson predicted that he would lose his strength and power, and he did.[10] Brides in waiting tend to grow their hair, and often insist that their attendants do so as well, so they can wear an up-do that later can be released and relaxed, with maybe a hint or more of sexual energy. Hair always tells a story.

The long and the short of it may have individual psychological meaning but it also may have biological and cultural meanings. Seen as a sign of youth, beauty, and health, long hair seems to be preferred by men. Perhaps the appeal has an evolutionary basis, representing reproductive potential or fertility.

Hair length intertwines with femininity and masculinity as these two comments reveal:

- "My hair tells people if I am feeling light and airy or a bit rigid. For many years I had long hair, then decided to cut it. I ended up cutting it so short that it was shorter than my husband's hair. I think I was feeling like I had to show my power through my manly cuts. Now, I have a softer look. I want to be softer as I grow older."
- "My hair length is very tied into my sexuality. My boyfriend sometimes wants me to pull it back, but that just doesn't feel sexy—I can't express myself the way I want to without being able to swing my hair around. Long hair is my key to feeling sexy and attractive."

Marie described the long and short of her hair over the years. While she always wanted long hair, her mother kept it short most of the time as it was easier to care for in their farming lifestyle. She recognizes that short hair made her mother feel competent and strong ("one of the boys") while it was more complicated for her especially as a teenager when she so wanted to be seen as feminine. Now, her husband's hair is longer than hers and she is trying to understand what that means to them as a couple:

Does hair and our relationship to it determine who we are and how we see ourselves? There is much discussion about the "size" of a certain appendage of men—do we as women and a society compare length of hair to determine our feminine nature? As my hair gets shorter and my husband's gets longer, do we cross over some magical divide? So, for today, my hair is growing. Tomorrow, who knows? Isn't that true about everything in life?

Darlene relates the ups and downs of her hair length:

In my youth, my hair was my glory. It was not cut for the first twelve years of my life and hung way below my waist—my mother praised it, my father adored it. It was thick, healthy and beautiful although it did tend a bit toward frizzing. To tame my locks, my mother tied it in rags most nights and then spent hours combing it out in the morning (and I was one of twelve children!). My hair was so long and thick that she had to use a steel-combed hairbrush to make her way through its mass. When I'd cry out in pain, my mom would smack the top of my head with the back of the brush and exclaim, "Beauties must suffer!"

Darlene begged to have her hair cut to avoid this pain and finally won, but then a new ritual began, one that, despite its discomfort, would be with her for years:

> Now I had to endure stinky permanent wave solutions torturing my sensitive scalp and sleeping on large, can-like rollers to tame the frizz. When hot rollers were introduced, I spent at least a half hour rolling my hair in excruciating heat (transferred to my scalp via the metal clips) every morning ... for the next 23 years! It must be noted, though, that I willingly participated in all of this without ever questioning its necessity. Family, friends, and culture had convinced me that my hair was *me*. If it was unkempt or lacked beauty that meant that I was unkempt and lacked beauty. Hair mattered *a lot* to me!

Next came breast cancer, chemotherapy, and a bagful of lost hair that became a transitional object until her hair grew back. "I was able to part with the saved bag once my hair hit my shoulders again. The importance of hair in my life had not waned ... my old 30-minute rolling ritual and the painful perms began anew."

But this deeply ingrained habit of curling her locks was interrupted by a tragic loss that reshaped Darlene's feelings about her hair once and for all.

> What I'd assumed to be a never-ending tradition ended abruptly after our younger daughter died unexpectedly at 19. About a year before her death, she'd taken me to a salon for a mother and daughter adventure. We sat in side-by-side beauty salon chairs for our hair makeovers. Hers turned out lovely. Mine, not so much. I'd ended up with the only new, inexperienced beautician in the place and she'd butchered my locks so badly that I had to return the next morning for repair. The owner of the salon apologetically trimmed my hair to above my ears in her attempt to "make it right." It felt nearly bald to me. It took quite a few weeks before I'd adjusted to my new look. Even so, I'd continued to painfully hot roll with a curling iron what was left on my head.
>
> I used to marvel at how my daughter could wash her hair in the morning, scrunch it with her fingers, and go. I envied her ease. After her death, taking time with my hair became unbearable. It seemed inconsequential, vain and a big waste of time. So I decided to try her approach. To my surprise, it worked. Chemotherapy had replaced my frizz with light curls and all it took was a bit of water, mousse and hand scrunching to discover my own wash and wear technique. I now spend about five minutes with my hair each morning. This feels far more balanced. When it comes down to what's important in life, hair is pretty much at the bottom of my list.

These hair stories prove that, like so many other important things in life, hair is all about relationships. Darlene finds solace in the hair rituals that she associates with the daughter she misses so much. Inevitably, what is deep in our hearts ends up on top of our heads. Hair is part of their ongoing connection and has a unique and profound meaning in her life.

"My anger was all over the place"

For Marisa (whose story is mentioned in Chapter 1, "Every Woman's Issue"), hair has spoken deep truths throughout her life and still does. Dramatic statements on top of her head announce each new era or stage in her life, culminating in impulsively shaving her head when she faced the decision to divorce her unfaithful husband. For her, very clearly, *hair tells a story*.

Hair had always been an emotional lightning rod in Marissa's life. The only sister of two brothers, her father constantly told her throughout her childhood that she was not as smart as they were, so she set her mind to be as boy-like as possible. Short hair became an important symbol of her desire to be seen as equal to her brothers. Trying to keep up with or outdo them, wrestling and fighting and denunciating anything "girly" had even resulted in hernia surgery when she was 11. As a teenager, Marissa wanted to let her hair grow, but her mother would not allow this, saying that her hair was thin and ugly and would not look good. During those awkward years, Marissa became ashamed of her changing body and constantly covered it up by wearing loose clothes and capes. Uncomfortable with her emerging femininity, Marissa finally had her first hairdresser appointment when she was 17, and, although she desperately wanted to let her hair grow, she decided to keep it short. The tomboy image felt protective to her.

Marissa envied the girls with their long hair and feminine style but felt this was impossible for her. Keeping her hair short, she gradually developed a strong, independent approach to life, accentuated with makeup and sexy clothes. She was trying hard to be sexy and feminine but never really felt like it. Her appearance made a statement but how others saw her and how she saw herself were probably two different things.

After she had her first child, Marisa grew her hair, as she felt more like a woman than she had ever before. She always wore it up to give the message that she was in control and not available sexually. Her mother's messages about her hair being flat and lifeless lingered and continued to shape her feelings about being a woman, all wrapped up in the hair on her head.

Things began to change dramatically for her after her second child was born. It was a traumatic and difficult birth, and she felt exhausted, depleted, and ugly afterward. Unfortunately, their mother's helper was a young woman with beautiful, lush hair and she sensed her husband's attraction to her. Before long, Marisa cut her hair short, once more announcing her pain and confusion. Within a few years, her hair was long again but again was the voice of her pain when her marriage began to fall apart. She explains:

> I was so devastated; powerless, betrayed and feeling stupid for having ignored what was going on for so long. I felt rejected, ugly, half of a woman, ashamed and guilty. One afternoon, I was on the phone with my mother-in-law, going on and on about my misery. She had to hang up for five minutes. By the time she called back, only a few minutes later, I had shaved my head. I was still in the bathroom, looking at my head and sensing that I had done something crazy, impulsive, and irrational. I thought of a nun, renouncing her life as a woman, as a sexual being. My husband had ignored my sexuality for five years. I had lived like a nun. I might as well look like one. I also thought of the women who had collaborated with the Nazis. Their heads were shaved, revealing to the world their betrayals. I was the one who had been betrayed and yet I was punishing myself. My anger was all over the place. I was very angry at myself. By mutilating myself I was probably expressing my failure as a woman, as a wife, and I deserved punishment.

Nearly 10 years later, Marisa's hair is long again but still the early negative experiences in her family affect how she feels about it and herself:

> I simply do not like my hair. I notice every day how flat, thin, straight and lifeless it is. No satisfaction, only annoyance, frustration, then resignation. Maybe because I am single now, it looks more sexy, inviting, attractive and younger. However, I do not like having my hair down. I am self-conscious of the way it hangs down flatly, with this obstinate separation line on top of

my head that makes me look like Jesus. When I wear it up, I feel like a severe schoolteacher. I have never felt joy or satisfaction with my hair.

Looking back at her life, Marissa realizes that her hair has always told the story about what is going on in her heart. Now when she is depressed, she tends to ignore it and to wash it only rarely; if this goes on very long, she develops dreadlocks, representing the blocks and snarls she feels in her life. I wonder what her hair will look like when she finds lasting peace within herself.

For most of us, life is full of snarls, tangles and transitions. Women often use their hair to mediate some of the stress or to reconnect to someone or some part of their earlier life. Whether conscious or subconscious, hair can often reveal deep truths and it is worth the time to figure these out. Hair always tells a story.

CHAPTER 13

"Good hair": The Dilemma of Non-White Hair in a White-Powered Culture

"Oppressed hair puts a ceiling on the brain."—Alice Walker[1]

"Good hair" isn't just about having a "good hair day." Unfortunately, in the United States, it is about being born with the kind of hair that most Caucasians have—that straight and manageable texture that has become the cultural standard for beauty. Those of us who have "good hair" tend to take it for granted, not understanding what power and status it instantly bestows on us. Those who do not have it are keenly aware of the difference.

Here are some harsh facts. When it comes to employment, in both the application and orientation processes, women of color are 30 percent more likely to be given formal grooming policies as conditions of employment. Clearly, hairstyles that reflect African American identity have historically been seen as less professional and less acceptable. No surprise, black and brown women generally do not feel comfortable showing their natural beauty and are 80 percent more likely to change their hair to meet workplace norms and expectations.[2]

We desperately need to address the follicular racism underlying the concept of "good hair."[3] In 2020, the United States finally began to confront the systemic racism that has been so apparent in our legal system after countless people of color—both men and women—have been killed by police in routine proceedings. Black Lives Matter has become a political movement and a belief shared by so many. Black hair also matters.

Hair as a Spiritual Barrier

The endless pursuit of "good hair" plagues women even as accomplished as Alice Walker, the first African American woman to win the Pulitzer Prize and the National Book Award for the highly acclaimed *The Color Purple.* After years of self-examination and contemplation, this spiritual leader and activist, one of the most accomplished women of modern times, recognized that her hair represented "the one last barrier to her spiritual liberation." She likened her hair to a rock that would forever limit her and anchor her spirit to the earth, unless she were to change her attitudes and treatment of it: "I realized that there was no hope of continuing my spiritual development, no hope of future growth of my soul ... if I still remained chained to thoughts about my hair. I suddenly understood why nuns and monks shaved their heads."[4]

Alice Walker's epiphany started her on a journey to reclaiming her hair after years of the oppression of processing. On the way to truly knowing and managing her own hair, she first chose to wear long braids, hair grown and sacrificed by Korean women to be sewn on the scalps of American women, including many African American women. She appreciated the skill, the art, and the dedication of her young hairdresser who would arrive at Walker's home with her young child at 7 in the evening and leave early in the morning hours.

She came to enjoy this ritual, deeply sensing a connection to ancient and ongoing African traditions. During this phase, her own hair was growing out beneath the braids, and gradually she was able to see its true springy, unpredictable nature for the first time at the age of 40. As she allowed her hair to grow, Walker felt that her spirit was once more growing and evolving in a way that her oppressed hair would never have allowed. She was then in control of her hair and her life. As she wrote: "The ceiling at the top of my brain lifted; once again my mind (and spirit) could get outside myself."

Only when Walker stopped fighting with her hair and trying to fit the image of "good hair" was she able to be her true self. This same story is echoed by many women of color and teaches us so much about the meaning hair can assume for any woman regardless of race or ethnicity.

Straight Hair Matters

Coming to the United States taught Chimamanda Ngozi Adichie, an award-winning novelist from Nigeria, the central role hair plays in the politics and power structure of American culture. As she says, "Black women's hair is political," telling us many other things about what matters in a culture. And straight hair matters.[5]

Chimamanda, author of the best seller *Americannah*, had never thought about herself as African or as Nigerian before arriving in the United States, but race and hair weigh heavily here. In contrast to her life in Nigeria, she witnessed countless assumptions being made about a black woman simply based on whether her hair was straight or not. In Chimamanda's experience in America, a natural hairstyle on a black woman somehow means she is anything from angry to deeply spiritual—maybe an artist or a vegetarian—all based on hair curl.

Hair figures prominently in Chimamanda's novels—almost like an additional central character. Ifemelu, *Americannah*'s main character, recently immigrated from Nigeria, is advised to take out her braids and straighten her hair before a job interview if she really wants the position. She plays the games she is supposed to with her hair, but then, regardless of her efforts to protect and condition it, her hair begins to fall out around the temples. Her friend advises that she cut her hair and go natural as she has, comparing hair processing to "being in prison. You're caged in. Your hair rules you.... You're always battling to make your hair do what it wasn't meant to do."[6]

Just as in real life, fictional Ifemelu's transition to natural hair is not smooth or easy, but in a few months, she adopted a TWA—Teeny Weeny Afro—and fell in love with it. As art imitates life, Ifemelu has much light to shed on the topic of hair, women, power, and racial politics.

"Good Hair" Isn't Just for Grown-Ups

When his three-year-old daughter shocked him by asking about how to get "good hair," the comedian and actor Chris Rock was inspired to understand what that really meant to her. After researching and visiting hair salons and talking to countless women across the country, Rock produced a popular documentary about the pressures African American women experience regarding their hair (*Good Hair*, 2009).[7] Disarmed by the question his little girl posed, Rock had no clue about the meaning and power that hair can have in women's lives. The movie is a poignant examination of critical social and cultural issues that African American women face every day, simply because their hair is different from the Caucasian standard. It has raised the consciousness of so many, regardless of the color of their skin or the nap of their hair, to the price we pay for seeing only straight Caucasian hair as "good hair."

After seeing this film, *Sesame Street*'s head writer and puppeteer Joey Mazzarino understood the struggle his daughter, adopted from Ethiopia, was already having at the age of four. She desperately wanted straight blond hair—just like her dolls. He wrote a song, "I Love My Hair," that has all the spirit and fun Sesame Street characters bring, starting with the sentiment "Don't need a trip to the beauty shop, because I love what I got on top." Throughout the video, the Muppet Segi brags about the many ways she can wear her hair: with a clip or a bow, in an Afro, up, down, all around, in barrettes or flying free. She changes her hairstyle many times in the video, just like many African American women do. This song is a celebration of non-white hair as well as a celebration of difference.[8]

The song instantly went viral on YouTube after its release in October 2010. All Mazzarino intended was to help his daughter to feel good about her hair, so he was shocked at the volume and passion of responses from countless women of all ages in need of the message that they could love their natural hair.

Another dad got into the effort to help black girls make peace with their natural hair, in fact winning the 2020 Oscar for animated short film. Matthew Cherry, a former NFL wide receiver, doing his daughter's hair for the first time, was inspired to use his new role in the film industry to create a story to address this dilemma. Matthew had long natural hair himself but was clueless about how to help his daughter get ready for "picture day" at school.

In *Hair Love*, the fictional character of Zuri's dad had to overcome his own feelings of inadequacy and invest time and energy in this important aspect of her life—an act of selfless love and pride. There was also a book by the same name. Boosted by a Kickstarter campaign, this touching, heartwarming, and consciousness-raising book landed on the New York Times Children's Bestseller list in 2019[9] and is also available on YouTube.[10] When a dad moves out of his comfort zone to understand his daughter's experience of her hair, he begins to rewrite the narrow, gendered narratives, especially important for African American and other marginalized families.

In the past few years, more African American women have been choosing to go natural. Surprisingly, Chris Rock, the Muppets, and now an Oscar-winning NFL wide receiver have helped this cause, raising our consciousness to the price women pay for the elusive "good hair."

Finally, we are making some progress in redefining beauty. In 2019, Zozibini Tunzi, a black woman from South Africa, defied advice that she wear a wig or a weave when competing for Miss Universe. She wore her hair natural and won that crown. Never believing she would win but desperately wanting black and brown girls to see themselves represented in pageants and other arenas that have not welcomed or acknowledged their contributions, she ignored every bit of advice she received.

Due to the timing of the global pandemic, Tunzi's reign as Miss Universe was the longest in the history of the pageant. That same year, the winners of all the major pageants in the U.S.—Miss America, Miss USA, Miss Teen USA and Miss World—were women of color[11] who sometimes showed their natural hair. Since "beauty contests" have historically reflected Eurocentric standards, this recognition of beauty in other skin tones, hair textures, races and ethnicities is long overdue. Brava!

> *"Of course, the most powerful, spectacular*
> *and glorious part of a Black woman's head is how we use it—*
> *the revolutionary way we love, the holistic way we organize,*
> *the creative way we make, protect and sustain life."*
> —MICHAELA ANGELA DAVIS[12]

"That's why I never learned to swim"

In a white-powered culture, non-white hair comes with a high cost, as Rosalie reveals:

It truly has had an enormous impact on my perception of myself and lack of "self-esteem." Growing up in the '60s as an African American girl, one who had a mother, aunts, and cousins with "straight hair" or, as we would say "good hair," which was white people's hair, hair that did not have to be straightened, was not only a physical situation, but an emotional one. To get your hair straightened as I did was a long process, a painful one. I did not mind my brown skin, but I did wish for straight hair, white people's hair, "good hair." I have much to tell.

Rosalie's *hair story* shows us that "good hair" is a lot more than the name of a movie—it is a cultural divide overvaluing Caucasian hair and diminishing the beauty and value of other ethnicities and races, causing tremendous implications and unrelenting pain for so many women.

I first met Rosalie through our shared passion for running. I am a dedicated runner, but she was a great runner, participating in countless races, even marathons. I admired her in many ways, not just for her athleticism, so I was shocked when she told me about her lifelong struggles with her hair. I shared with her the research that African American women often do not exercise as much as recommended in order to avoid messing the hair to which they have devoted so much time and money. Instantly Rosalie told me, "That's why I never learned to swim." My heart broke, standing outside in the sunshine on a very hot summer day, when this wonderful woman and accomplished athlete explained that her mother would never allow her to learn to swim because she spent so much time straightening her hair

135

each week and "swimming would ruin everything." So, this athlete, who has worn her hair cropped as short as possible for decades as an adult, still has not learned to swim. At that moment I learned the true cost of wanting "good hair."

Another African American woman immediately described how water had been the enemy of her hair throughout her childhood. Lauren was not allowed to wash her own hair till she was in sixth grade, when she and some friends were given strict instructions of what products they needed and how to approach this task at a special sleepover. Like Rosalie, she and her female cousins had never been taught to swim, but all her male cousins were swimmers. During trips to the beach, with their mothers sitting on the shore, their fathers and other male family members spent hours swimming. The girls could only play in the sand. They were allowed to get their feet wet—but never their hair. She used the exact same words: "Swimming would ruin everything."

Before she was even old enough for school, Lauren recounts that her mother brought her three daughters to the salon every two weeks to get their hair chemically straightened. Not all African American hair is the same in terms of texture, kink or curl, and her mother's hair was actually straight and easy to manage, quite different from that of Lauren and her sisters. She did not have any experience with the kind of hair her daughters had, so the family invested significant amounts of time and money at the salon. The girls had to guard their hair like gold in between these visits. She remembers an endless list of excuses to keep her from participating in gym at school. Although she knew lying was not right, ruining her hair would be far worse. It was a necessary trade-off. At the age of 35, Lauren, for the very first time, allowed her hair to be natural. It has been an adventure full of surprises, and so far, she is enjoying it.

"When my hair went, my freedom started"

Another woman of color described her many years of struggling with her hair. The community in which Darcy grew up held the

136

unspoken value: "the lighter the skin and the better the hair, the better off you were." To this day Darcy remembers her mother's reaction when, at four years old, she washed her own hair with Dial soap. Her mom spent a chunk of time each week combing and braiding her hair, often a very painful process, and washing it spontaneously when Mom was out and Dad was not paying attention did not go over well. Darcy learned to never do that again and spent years with chemically relaxed hair, first done by her mom and later in salons. She gradually felt more in charge of her hair but was always having it chemically processed. Finally, after starting a family, she decided she no longer could devote the time to this.

> What a constraint my hair had been for me. It took so much time. I had to plan to wash and braid or treat it or have someone else do it. I never realized how much pain was associated with my hair. Frankly, I was tired of the burns. I had it cut all the way down and now I feel my natural beauty comes out. I don't cover it. I don't change it. With earrings and jewelry, I can jazz up my look, but now I appreciate my head—people comment on it, sometimes rub it. This is the style I'll die in. This is what I was meant to be. When my hair went, my freedom started. I'm becoming an athlete, swimming, and running and playing tennis—things I wouldn't do before. This is me and I finally love myself.

Darcy never fully loved or accepted herself until she rid herself of all the fussing about her hair, only then recognizing the toll it had taken. She has already decided that she will let her cropped hairdo naturally go salt and pepper as time goes by—the freedom from chemical treatment and time in the hair salon feels too good to give up.

"I took my wig off because
I no longer wanted to apologize for who I am."
—Viola Davis[13]

The African American community is conflicted on this topic. In fact, transitioning to more natural hair is not easy after years of straightening and relaxing treatments. It takes time to learn how to manage natural curl and kink as well as a lot of costly products. So, while many espouse a natural look, they do not necessarily choose this for themselves. Similarly, some salons promoted as natural may not offer chemical straightening or weaves but still do a lot of color processing. Non-white hair in a white-powered culture is a challenge.

Hair and Health

The financial investment women of color make in hair care is startling—exceeding $500 billion annually on hair care and grooming products in the United States alone. In fact, according to consumer research in the UK, women of color spend six times what their white peers spend.[14] And, after investing money and time this way, women of color often say they exercise less than they should because they worry about ruining their hairstyle. For some, hair is a (not-so) subtle form of slavery and disempowerment.

Even former U.S. surgeon general Dr. Regina Benjamin has stressed the critical role hair plays in the lives of African American women. With her own mother a hairstylist, she grew up knowing the positive influence a hair professional can have. In fact, current research shows that African Americans are more likely to pay attention to their health and even to see their physicians when hairstylists are pushing them to be proactive about these issues! Dr. Benjamin highlighted increased physical fitness as one of her primary goals for the country, but she acknowledges that for women, especially African American women, wanting to avoid disrupting their hair keeps them from regular rigorous exercise.[15]

In a study of African American women done at Wake Forest Baptist Medical Center, 40 percent admitted that concerns about their hair keep them from exercising. Sweating introduces that disruptive moisture, so they tend to avoid rigorous aerobic exercises, despite the recommendation that adults exercise intensely for approximately 150 minutes per week. Like many women of color, in this study, more than 60 percent report that they use chemical products to straighten their hair. Not only time consuming, the chemicals also make their hair more fragile and apt to break if washed or manipulated too often. Regardless of the health risks associated with a sedentary lifestyle (hypertension, diabetes, and cardiovascular disease), 26 percent of the women in this study do not exercise at all. The good news is that 50 percent of the participants said they had changed their hairstyle to allow them to exercise.[16]

The surgeon general asked women to risk a bad hair day to assure a longer, stronger, and healthier life. Hair tells a story, and Dr. Benjamin wants it to be less about appearance and more about health. The real answer is about more than tolerating a "bad hair day." Instead, we must redefine beauty to include every kind of hair and hairdo and come up with products to minimize the impact of sweat or to protect sensitive scalps or dry hair from damaging chemicals like the chlorine in pools. In the meantime, Brava to the former surgeon general for adding hair to her list of concerns when it comes to women's well-being.

By the way, although the stakes are not as high, white women also use the excuse "But I just got my hair done." We all need to find ways to integrate healthy habits with our hair care and other appearance issues.

Important Issues That We Can Ignore No Longer

Racial discrimination, exclusion, and oppression were all alive and well at the 2021 Olympic Games swimming competition. And hair was part of this ugly reality. Chlorine dries out and damages everyone's hair, but its impact on hair with the texture and kink of many women of color is far worse. Traditional swim caps are so tight and small that they offer little help, simply not fitting the usual volume and thick curl of a swimmer with natural kinky hair.

A British company, Soul Cap, created a swim cap that can accommodate natural hair in time for the 2021 games, but the organization that oversees international water sports competitions (Fédération Internationale De Natation or FINA) rejected it. Swimmers should not have to choose between the health of their hair and the chance to compete nor should black and brown women have to give up this central aspect of their identity and self-expression. As Dawn Butler, a member of the British Parliament stated, this is "discrimination in plain sight."[17] Once again, hair is more than just hair.

Soul Cap and the athletes advocating for inclusion and competing in swimming did not stop. FINA finally approved the use of Soul Cap in 2022, a year after the games. We need to continue to do all we can to make sports available to all regardless of race, ethnicity, class, and hair! This is especially important when it comes to swimming, considering the significant health and safety risks of not being able to swim. It really is a life and death issue.

Systemic racism underlies decisions about exercise as well as access to physical or athletic opportunities. Hair alone does not keep women of color from exercising. For far too long, public swimming pools, beaches and access to water have been segregated and off limits to families of color. Many had no opportunities to learn to swim and therefore could not teach their children. This is a serious public health problem that has been ignored for far too long. We need to address this and make swimming and water activities available and safe for everyone.

CHAPTER 14

From the Roots to the CROWN

"If your hair is relaxed, white people are relaxed. If your hair is nappy, they're not happy."—Paul Mooney[1]

Today's decisions about natural versus straight hair are not cosmetic—they are deeply rooted in the historical context of race and power in the United States. We would love to erase the enslavement of people of color from our history, but we cannot. Nor can we erase it from our attitudes toward hair. For African Americans, hair has been central to attempts both to assimilate into the dominant white culture and to distinguish themselves from it. The history of race relations in the United States is in itself a hair story—and not a pretty one.

Enslaved Africans arrived in North America in 1619, the same time that white women first arrived from Europe. As shameful as this is, soon laws were enacted to institutionalize enslavement and take away any rights of blacks. By the early 1700s, they could only be enslaved and had no personal freedom. They were worked to the bone, literally and figuratively, and had little time to groom, despite the importance hair had historically played in African culture. Some traders shaved the heads of the enslaved to disempower and disconnect them further from their traditions. Others plucked any gray hair or dyed the hair a deep black to make the enslaved person appear younger and more valuable on the market.[2]

Instead of the ornate and symbolic hair they wore in Africa, the enslaved in America often just wore scarves or rags to cover and control their hair. Scalp diseases, ringworm, lice, and other problems

141

routinely caused infections and hair loss. Those who had a closer relationship with their owners, like the housekeepers, cooks, nurse-maids, and valets, had somewhat more comfortable working conditions and tended to wear their hair like their owners did or to style neat braids and cornrows similar to African traditions. But if threatened by an attractive house slave, the mistress of the home might order the hair to be chopped off. Workers with lighter skin and straighter hair often were favored, creating long lasting associations between hair and self-worth subconsciously internalized by both whites and blacks. Hair always seems to be a target of emotion—and a weapon of power.

In the 19th century, laws allowed enslaved people to have Sundays free from work, giving a day for rest, religious activities, and grooming. Having gotten the message loud and clear that straight hair was preferred in this culture, on those precious Sundays, many began to experiment with ways to relax their hair,[3] using products like lye, which also burned any skin it touched. Nappy or kinky hair was a problem to overcome, not a natural resource to cherish or even to just accept. This attitude toward hair continued after enslavement was abolished, as blacks met ongoing discrimination, distrust, hatred, and maltreatment.

"Eventually I knew what hair wanted; it wanted to be itself ... to be left alone by anyone, including me, who did not love it as it was."
—ALICE WALKER[4]

For these women, hair gradually became a way to assimilate and to improve the status of all African Americans. Straight hair represented the dominant Eurocentric view of beauty. In 1896, the National Association of Colored Women, formed initially to protest lynching and other human rights violations, soon began to emphasize grooming and appearance as a means of improving relations.[5] Lighter skin and straighter hair were highly desired, and chemicals could help to achieve both. The pressure was on African American women to fight old stereotypes and to show the worth of their race—what better way than through their hair, something for everyone to see?

142

In the 20th century, the Black Power Movement of the 1960s changed some attitudes toward hair and beauty. The "Afro" arrived, but soon a more conservative mood set in again, and hair relaxers ruled once more. One African American studies scholar even suggested that "nappy" became the other, maybe more acceptable "N-word." Just as they did with "nigger," whites began using the word "nappy" to degrade black people.[6]

Where We Are Today

Hair is a powerful medium of self-expression, power and autonomy and continues to evolve in the 21st century. Sales of hair straightening kits declined by 38 percent between 2012 and 2017, with black hair care expanding steadily each year, to an estimated annual value of $2.5 billion in 2018.[7] The sales of relaxers dropped 25 percent in a recent five-year period, with some estimates suggesting that, by 2019, sales of hair relaxers declined to 45 percent of what they were at their peak.[8]

Although fewer women are using chemical relaxers, the sales of wigs, weaves, extensions, and braids have increased dramatically. Over half of black and brown women wear some sort of weave or extension, allowing them to not only switch looks but also to give their hair a break from chemical treatments.[9]

Unfortunately, the switch from chemical treatments to weaves and extensions is not all good news. Recently, based on a review of 19 studies, researchers at Johns Hopkins University School of Medicine warned about the risk of permanent hair loss from wearing weaves, braids, and hair extensions as they are often wrapped or attached too tightly, pulling on the hair follicles. Some are even glued on. The result is traction alopecia, which now occurs disproportionately in African American women. The risk for traction alopecia is higher when the scalp hair has been chemically treated as it is already stressed and less able to tolerate the pulling on the roots. Unprocessed and untreated hair is healthier from the start so can withstand some abuse. The damage to the scalp can be decreased and even prevented with careful attention and less use of glues and chemical and thermal straightening techniques. Dermatologists recommend that braids be loosened and not in place longer than two to three months. Weaves and extensions should be removed at six to eight weeks.[10]

Not only do these hair techniques cost a woman some hair and some significant physical and emotional discomfort, they also can cost a lot of cash. Ironically, choosing a hairstyle to improve self-confidence and self-esteem and to minimize chemical exposure can end up causing damage to the hair and scalp as well as to the wallet.

Estimates indicate that African Americans spent as much as $500 billion, approximately half of their expendable income, on hair care and related products in 2009, with this increasing steadily each year.[11] Extensions can cost as little as $300 or as much as $10,000, depending on the region of the country and the exact service and technique. Touchups are necessary every four to six weeks, because the natural hair underneath continues to grow. Changing to a "hair system" can cost from $4,000 to $80,000 a year, excluding the time away from work, travel, and expenses like babysitting if young children are part of the picture. Despite the expense, some girls start experimenting with weaves and braids as early as high school.

This is a concern for many reasons, especially since it keeps money away from other causes that might help African Americans more. When it comes to grooming and beauty products, women of color may spend as much as nine times more than the average consumer here in the United States.[12] The bottom line is that "fashion fabulous hair" can reflect the deep desire to be accepted by our dominant, white-powered culture and to satisfy its beauty standards. Once more, an attempt to empower may actually serve to disempower women.

"Hair product use is likely an important culprit
of environmental health disparities
in African-American women compared to white women."
—TAMARRA JAMES-TODD[13]

Risky Business for Both Clients and Stylists

According to a 2018 report in *Scientific American*, toxic chemicals are found in countless beauty products, posing risks for all women, but hair products developed and marketed to women of color are the worst.[14] The health risks associated with these chemicals—breast cancer, neurological disorders, learning disabilities, reproductive and endocrine irregularities, and respiratory issues—occur disproportionately in black women. Some of the products contain placenta, linked to both breast cancer and early puberty. Related to the earlier onset of puberty, African American girls suffer a higher rate of invasive breast cancer and a greater mortality risk.

Chemicals known to be endocrine disruptors were found in half of the hair products used commonly by black American women but only in 7 percent of those used by Caucasian American women. Endocrine disruptors do just that: they interfere with the normal development and functioning of the endocrine system which regulates critical reproductive and other biological processes. Readily absorbed by skin and inhalation, some of these chemicals—preservatives and plasticizers that make products creamy and easy to apply—have been banned in Europe but are still marketed in the United States for everyday use and are even in products targeted at children. Many of the ingredients are the same as those that are found in cleaning products, depilatories, drain cleaners, and even embalming fluid, although they may be labeled differently. The companies involved are known to change the names of the ingredients and do whatever they can to confuse or deceive any attempts to regulate them.

In light of the many health disparities affecting people of color living in the United States—racism, food insecurity, housing insecurity, police brutality and the criminal justice system, to name a few—adding these risks is frightening. Comprehensive government regulation of the hair products marketed to women, as well as consumer education, are compelling needs. This is social justice—and medical justice—in action.

Napptural Beauty

Her own painful experiences with her hair led Patricia "Dee-coily" Gaines to create Nappturality.com, the largest natural hair website on the Internet. After harsh relaxers damaged and broke her hair, Gaines felt forced to wear weaves and wigs, then began to braid her hair as it grew in and gradually transitioned to dreadlocks. Life without chemical relaxers was liberating, but when she wanted to take her locks down, her stylist advised a relaxer again. Searching for ways to wear her hair natural—other than in locks or in an Afro—Gaines found little help and too much typing of hair as good or bad. Soon, she and a few others started sharing their experiences on webpages and Nappturality.com evolved.[15] "Napptural" stands for Afro-type hair that is worn natural, with no straightening or chemical relaxing, and is worn visibly, celebrating its natural texture, and not covered up by a wig, a weave, or extensions.

Gaines is not only trying to promote napptural hair. She also wants us to question and transform the beliefs we have about non-straight hair, what she calls the "3-U myth." Starting with the myth that black hair is *ugly, unmanageable, and undesirable*, she counters that black hair is actually *underestimated, undervalued, and unloved* and challenges us to see black hair as *unique, urbane, and utopian*.[16] Brava!

Hair Discrimination

Hair rights are fundamental human rights. Anyone who questions if hair really is an issue in modern American culture can google "hair discrimination" and literally millions of hits will appear (222,000,000 on December 20, 2021). One of the first is a definition from the NAACP Legal Defense Fund: "Hair discrimination is rooted in systemic racism, and its purpose is to preserve white spaces. Policies that prohibit natural hairstyles, like afros, braids, bantu knots, and locs, have been used to justify the removal of Black children from classrooms, and Black adults from their employment. With no nationwide legal protections against hair discrimination, Black people are often left to risk facing consequences at school or work for their natural hair or invest time and money to conform to Eurocentric professionalism and beauty standards."[17]

Hair discrimination targets people of color, who have not had their hair chemically straightened. Especially for African Americans, hair has power and meaning, and unfortunately, it can be—and often is—used against them. This has prompted countless lawsuits, ACLU cases and new legislation in a growing number of states to guard against discrimination based on hair. Every human being has the right to their hair.

Dreadlocks or Cultural Dread of Racial Equality?

In 2010, the Equal Employment Opportunity Commission (EEOC) filed a lawsuit that alleged that Chastity Jones, a black woman, had suffered racial discrimination when an employer rescinded a job offer because she refused to cut her dreadlocks.[18] The potential employer had a policy stating that an employee's "hairstyle should reflect a business/professional image" and that "[n]o excessive hairstyles or unusual colors are acceptable." The human resources manager told her they could not hire her "with the dreadlocks." The EEOC suit proposed that race encompasses "cultural characteristics related to race or ethnicity," such as "grooming practices," and that "dreadlocks are nonetheless a racial characteristic, just as skin color is a racial characteristic."

The U.S. District Court judge disagreed, dismissing the lawsuit, and later refused to hear an appeal asserting that the EEOC did not prove intentional racial discrimination. In the end, after other legal maneuvers, the EEOC did not bring the case to the Supreme Court. Subsequently, the NAACP Legal Defense and Education Fund (LDF) filed a motion asking the court to allow the original individual plaintiff to intervene and appeal the case to the Supreme Court. This was also refused. The attempt to ban this form of racial discrimination was lost as employers were allowed to continue to ban natural hairstyles.

Over the years as this case was being considered (2010–2018), many other instances of racial discrimination based on natural hair emerged in the popular press and in court cases. For example, in 2017, a charter school outside Boston punished African American high school girls with multiple detentions for wearing braided extensions, asserting they violated the dress code.[19] A New Jersey case that captured national attention concerned a 16-year-old mixed-race wrestler who was forced to cut his dreadlocks or forfeit his match. The referee gave him only 90 seconds to decide and the young man conceded to this pressure. Andrew Johnson had been complying with regulations requiring his hair to be covered, but this sudden ultimatum was a complete surprise. The referee has since lost his job at that school system.[20]

In 2020, DeAndre Arnold, a high school senior in Texas, received notification from his school that he would not be allowed to walk with his class at graduation unless he cut his dreadlocks off. He had been wearing locks for years, loyally following the strict dress code which requires hair above the earlobes, off the shoulders, and out of the eyes. He had respected these rules throughout his high school career and never let his hair down at school but was given no choice but to cut them off to be able to "walk," the highly valued tradition marking the end of the secondary school experience and moving forward in life. His family is from Trinidad where the custom is for men to grow their hair and wear locks. DeAndre's hairstyle shows reverence for both family and cultural traditions and should be honored.[21]

After this story was reported in national news, many people—including prominent athletes and entertainers—supported DeAndre. Ellen DeGeneres invited him to appear on her show when she announced that she and Alicia Keys have given him a $20,000 scholarship. He and his parents were guests at the Oscars, invited by Matthew Cherry and the team that created *Hair Love* (see Chapter 13), the animated film encouraging African American girls to love their hair. Although the school district had voted to uphold its policy, months later, a judge in the U.S. District Court for the Southern District of Texas ruled that the policy was discriminatory, depriving him and other students of an equal education.[22] Hair has been a powerful tool for racism. Finally, that is beginning to change.

"Hair is never just hair. It's culture. It's pride.... I own it.
I'm proud of it.... For Black women,
it's really about culture and identity."
—Connecticut state senator Marilyn Moore
at the Passage of the CROWN Act in Connecticut[23]

The CROWN Act (Create a Respectful and Open Workplace for Natural Hair)

Without the U.S. Supreme Court being willing to recognize that hair policies can be examples of racial discrimination, racism continues, as seen in these stories, severely limiting the opportunities of all people of color, male and female. In response to the lack of federal action, state and local entities have begun to develop laws promoting racial equality by limiting the implicit and explicit bias allowed by grooming and hair policies with a legislative initiative creatively called the CROWN Act (Create a Respectful and Open Workplace for Natural Hair). The mission of the CROWN Coalition—a partnership of Dove, the National Urban League, Color of Change, and the Western Center on Law and Poverty—is to prohibit race-based hair discrimination. It will ban the denial of employment and educational opportunities because of hair texture or protective hairstyles including braids, locs, twists or bantu knots.[24] Hair discrimination affects all genders. As in so many issues, all genders deserve better and more equitable treatment.

In July of 2019, California was the first state to pass a law to prohibit discrimination based on hair style and hair texture. New York and New Jersey soon followed, the New Jersey statute becoming law on December 19, 2019, the exact anniversary of the wrestling match during which Andrew Johnson's dreadlocks were cut. Since then, more states have joined the effort to end follicular racism, including Colorado, Connecticut, Delaware, Illinois, Louisiana, Maine, Maryland, Massachusetts, Nebraska, Nevada, New Jersey, New Mexico, New York, Oregon, Tennessee, Vermont, Virginia, and Washington while individual cities have passed similar bills. Federal legislation is also in the works. In September 2020, the House of Representatives passed the CROWN Act, paving the way for federal protection, if the Senate also votes to approve it. Once enacted, characteristic traits historically associated with race, such as hair texture and hairstyle, would be fully protected from discrimination in the workplace and in government sponsored institutions such as K–12 public and charter schools.

The Crown Coalition has also proposed a Black Hair Independence Day or National Crown Day to be celebrated every July 3. This would be a day of solidarity and celebration for the human rights and hair rights of all people of color. Quite simply, time is up. The Crown Act could be the catalyst we need to equalize opportunity and end a major source of race-based prejudice.

Prior to the New York state initiative, the New York City Human Rights Commission passed an amendment to their Human Rights Law, protecting the right to wear "natural hair, treated or untreated hairstyles such as locks, cornrows, twists, braids, Bantu knots, fades, Afros, and/or the right to keep hair in an uncut or untrimmed state."[25] These laws or amendments, as important as they are, only apply to public institutions, not to religious institutions such as Catholic schools that serve many non-white students. In fact, countless Catholic schools have fostered Eurocentric grooming policies that convey a bias against any hairstyles associated with racial identity, subtly and not so subtly, suggesting that white culture is the blessed culture and the one most closely associated with God.

A thought-provoking article in the *National Catholic Reporter* proposes that theology and ethics are the only way to reverse the devaluation of African American culture and the strict Eurocentric expectations and regulations for grooming and appearance. Public laws do not apply to religious institutions but delineating and respecting the church's basic teachings about God's love and the importance of diversity and acceptance could begin a true healing process. To Maria Teresa Davila, associate professor of Christian ethics at Andover Newton Theological School, the ongoing pattern of policing black students' hair represents a vestige of America's racial segregation, a new variation of the public hygiene codes that were imposed on black people.

Pope Francis, the current leader of the Catholic Church, has been adamantly anti-racist in his preaching and writing. So far, however, this has not translated into noticeable change—ongoing bias against natural hairstyles persists in many Catholic schools. While at higher levels, the importance of cultural sensitivity may be discussed and promoted, the actual administrators who develop and enforce school policies have ignored the fact that the policing of black people's hair has historically been used as a weapon against them.

Each time an African American is judged, marginalized, sent home, or expelled—as in school cases—that individual is ostracized and deeply hurt. We must remember that these cases are real people with real feelings. C. Vanessa White, professor of spirituality and ministry at Catholic Theological Union in Chicago, describes it well: "The child is made to feel there is something wrong with them. And that's a trauma that can't be erased."[26] The cost of this ongoing racism is both systemic and individual. Both are serious violations of human dignity. Once more, hair rights are human rights.

The Right to Choose

Like many other women, I dream of a culture that elevates all kinds of beauty—and hair—and sees people as equal, all deserving the same rights, dignity, and respect, regardless of economic power, ethnicity, gender, or skin color. Although we are far from that goal, it is important to be honest about where we stand and to keep working toward this goal.

More than anything else, women of every race should be able to make their own choices about their hair. Right now, black and brown women cannot win. If they straighten their hair, they can be criticized for "selling out." If they go natural, they are criticized for being too political or not doing enough to meet beauty standards. Both decisions have consequences. Constant chemical treatment of hair and use of hot combs can permanently damage the hair follicle and cause hair loss. Burns from heat and chemicals and the traction on the scalp from tightly sewn weaves are painful. Research also suggests a potential link between relaxers and uterine fibroids and early puberty.[27] Damage to our reproductive systems is a frightening prospect, but as the FDA does not regulate hair care products like these, we know very little about the long-term health consequences.

While those issues have a cost, the historical abuse and disempowerment associated with natural hair also comes with a price. When C.J. Walker created the hot comb, black women felt they had no choice: to be able to work, and put food on the table, they had to tame their hair. As recently as 2007, when an editor from *Glamour* magazine advised a large Manhattan law firm about the "dos and don'ts" of corporate fashion, the message was essentially that the Afro is a definite "no-no" and that dreadlocks were "dreadful." In her opinion, natural hair and the office could not co-exist—natural hair is just too "political" a statement and therefore a risky business practice.[28] The law firm's managing partner, who happened to be a white man, discounted the advice when he heard it, and no policies were instituted about hair, but the fact that this kind of advice was still given in the 21st-century workplace is alarming.

To Professor Ingrid Banks, author of *Hair Matters: Beauty, Power, and Black Woman's Consciousness*,[29] having a choice is the critical issue, not the actual hairstyle. Reminding us that enslaved plantation workers never had that luxury, she sees any decision black women make today, from relaxing their hair, to cutting it off, or allowing it to be entirely free and natural, as empowering. She is right. It is time to accept women's decisions about their hair and their bodies as their right—and theirs alone. But it is also time to eradicate the racism, sexism, and rigid beauty standards that underlie our complicated relationship with our hair. And it is time that we all know the true health risks of the various hair products marketed to us. Only then will our decisions really be free.

CHAPTER 15

Hairapy or Therapy?
Stylists as Essential Workers

"Every appointment is like a short story, with a beginning, a middle, and an end. But the story never ends, really. Because every six weeks, or two months, or twice a year ... the story picks up where it was left off, like a never-ending series of sequels."—Kate Bollick[1]

Hair is a complicated subject, and so are the relationships we have with the people we trust to care for it. Clients come in, at the least hoping to rid themselves of the stress of life, and, at the most, seeking a complete transformation—physically, emotionally, maybe even spiritually. That is quite an agenda for one hair appointment. Many women see their stylist, be it a professional or someone less formal, as an intrinsic element in their self-care. With the COVID pandemic interfering with this aspect of life, some of us have come to perceive stylists and hair care professionals as "essential workers" who should be valued and protected just as other essential workers are.

The art of hairstyling entails a complex interplay of abilities and personal qualities that not everyone has. Minimally, good stylists possess "people skills" like emotional intelligence, patience, intuition, and a steel-trap memory to recall the minuscule details of our lives. As in any service industry, they need to accept all kinds of people and must be eager to keep learning as new styles, trends, techniques, and products are always emerging. Of course, skilled hands, spatial awareness, imagination, and creativity are essential. An intuitive sense for angles and geometry helps immensely. Plus, they must have the stamina to stand on their feet all day, work long hours, and be as flexible as Gumby to respond to their clients' scheduling needs. The working conditions are not easy, especially as stylists age. (Watch out for joint pain, sore feet and hands, and hope that arthritis is not around the corner!) A strong business sense also will help to build a client base and assure a good living. Job growth trends as projected by the Bureau of Labor Statistics suggest stronger growth for hair care professionals than any other career—19 percent growth between 2020 and 2030, in contrast to the average increase of approximately 8 percent.[2] That is good news for anyone aspiring for a career in the hair industry.

In the United States, each state has its own specific training requirements for licensing, but all mandate that aspiring hair professionals must be 16 years or older and graduate from cosmetology or beauty school, most of which require a high school diploma or equivalency. Classes include cutting, styling, coloring, and chemical treatments as well as the science of hair, basics of safety and sanitation, and some business issues. The training is generally nine months or longer, including a certain number of hours devoted to practice, with a formal exam before licensing. Some two-year programs at community colleges grant an associate degree. After this, hair professionals often seek specialized training in areas such as color or extensions, with certificates either from companies making the products or from professional organizations.[3]

Despite these many requirements and likely pressures, a study of occupational stress levels ranked hairdressing as less demanding than I would expect. Diagnostic medical sonographers reported the least stress, and hairstylists ranked second. Professionals in these two careers generally do not work in the public eye or in imminently risky environments, nor do they usually face high travel demands or deadlines, all of which increase occupational stress.[4]

Yet hair stylists have to deal with clients all day with few opportunities to escape and they are constantly exposed to chemicals, which may have some long-term effects. (See Chapter 13.) The creativity, spirit, and artistry of fellow stylists, plus the fact that most clients are happy to be there, may counter those stressors. After all, a client's experience in the hair chair is a world apart from sitting in a dental chair. (Apologies to my father and all dentists.) And most salons create a positive, upbeat environment with music and décor and even drinks and snacks (pre-pandemic, that is).

According to one survey, hairdressers are the fifth most trusted professionals in the UK. Responding to that data, stylist Nina Pottell commented, "hairdressing is about so much more than what I can do with my scissors and comb."[5] She is right—hair is never just hair and hairstyling has never been just about the styling. My conversations with women across the country and with stylists echo that message.

From Medicine Men to Salons and Stylists

As mentioned in Chapter 3, the precursors of today's stylists were medicine men and priests, gradually coming to be called barbers. Back in the day, people believed in good and evil spirits that gained entry to a person through their hair. The barber became a focal point in the community as legend had it that he could drive the evil away simply by cutting the individual's hair. Over time, barbers became known for their spiritual and religious beliefs, even performing marriages and baptisms. In ceremonies to rid people of evil, their hair would hang down loose while dancing and then be pulled back tightly so the good spirits would remain and no more evil spirits could come in.[6]

Barbers did far more than attend to the hair on the head. They also functioned as surgeons and dentists, performing operations, extracting teeth, and doing treatments like bloodletting and leeching. Known as barber surgeons, they formed an organization as early as the year 1094, with the now well-known striped barber pole as its symbol, representing surgery with red and hairdressing with white. Barbers were paid well, more than a surgeon would receive. These legends and practices are the predecessors of today's stylists. No wonder hair is such a complicated part of our lives and the relationship with our stylists can be so complex and meaningful.

Professional hair services provided by barbers and in shops are largely a gender-based phenomenon. By the Middle Ages, hair care for men was a formal business, and by the late 19th and early 20th centuries, most hair services took place at a barbershop or in a similar setting. However, women's hair care usually took place at home, often done by servants or family or friends—only certain people were allowed to touch a woman's hair. In fact, the Catholic church specifically forbade men touching women's hair. During the late 19th century, these customs began to loosen, and hair salons came into being, first in Paris.[7] Now nearly 900,000 salons operate in the United States,[8] although home hair care is still prevalent—and increasingly so during the pandemic.

Just as the barbershop was a central gathering place for men, the salon became that same hub for women, with sharing of life stories, community issues, resources, and advice about everything—from sex and birth control to childrearing and job opportunities. Conversations there tend to be intimate and honest, as a salon is a safe place for many, although it also can become a hotbed for gossip with the wrong mix of clients. Shared concerns about community issues sometimes lead customers to decide to take some action, to do something to help solve the problems they identified. For example, back in the 1930s, the Great Depression affected so many families in the United States, devastating their incomes and endangering their well-being from the emotional to the basics of food insecurity. Hair salons became rallying places for philanthropic efforts to keep families afloat.[9] These traditions have continued to this day.

"Hair is a microcosm of different issues in America today."
—MYKA HARRIS, BEAUTY ENTREPRENEUR[10]

Despite all the good that salons and stylists do each day, the truth is that the hair business has been segregated along gender and racial lines, mirroring our culture. Hair salons are highly segregated, with many white stylists having little if any skill or training in working with natural hair. In fact, such instruction and guidance has not been routinely included in cosmetology schools or textbooks.[11] This is a serious gap reflecting the enormous impact of institutional racism. Over the past century, women of color have begun to develop their own businesses to answer the specific needs of their natural hair.

Throughout my adult life, I have been fortunate to have my hair care provided in settings that have been integrated, both for gender and for race. I wish we had less segregation and more unity in the U.S. hair business. Hair tells the story of our culture's divisions too well. Let us all work for change.

Relational Hair Care

To many women, the relationship with their hairdresser is as important as that with their healthcare provider or their therapist. Some hairdressers in fact play the role of therapist, seeing us multiple times each year, often each month, sometimes even weekly, and over the course of many years. Like the proverbial bartender, they listen to our stories and never seem to judge. They have ideas and resources for us, as their last client just mentioned a great new restaurant, a dependable plumber, or the best medical specialist for whatever ails you. A stylist is like a life coach in many ways, helping us find our strengths and weaknesses and overcome the things that hold us back from reaching our goals.

"I think the most important thing a woman can have—
next to talent, of course—is her hairdresser."
—JOAN CRAWFORD[12]

Hairstylists tend to be rich resources of information but also of empathy—as a psychotherapist I understand that it is quite an art to listen without judgment. Every hairstylist I have known does that to the ultimate degree. Over the years of research for this book, however, I did hear a few stories of non-empathic hairdressers whose blunders or insensitivity always ended the relationship.

Francine told me that she had not felt satisfied with her stylist for years, but they were related so she felt obligated to stay with her. One day, as they got to the moment when the stylist turns the chair so the client can see the finished product, Francine saw that her stylist was looking at her own image and not at her. This was the tipping point. Francine had felt "not seen" for a long time but tolerated it due to the complicated nature of their relationship. That day she walked away, vowing to never again put up with feeling ignored, realizing that she deserved more than what she was receiving in many relationships. It was a liberating and empowering moment for her and truly changed her life—not just her relationship with her stylist. This epiphany led her not only to be more assertive and direct but also to expect more of others—all due to acknowledging that she felt so invisible to her stylist.

For some women, a male hairdresser is one of the longest and most stable relationships with a man she is likely to have. Clients enjoy undivided attention often for an hour or more and are free to talk about anything the way they might to a partner or a best friend, but with no strings attached. And stylists also let clients into their lives—it is a surprisingly complex, deep, and mutual relationship that both participants often come to honor and enjoy. Hair connects us to ourselves and to other people.

Hairapy

You won't find the word hairapy in a traditional dictionary, but a Google search yields more than 140,000 responses (December 2021), including names of salons and hair products, but most women know what the word means instantly. The top definition (i.e., the most popular) in the Urban Dictionary online defines hairapy as "going to get your hair done as a form of therapy that is especially effective when your hairdresser listens unconditionally and doesn't hand out stupid advice."[13] Having practiced psychotherapy for more than four decades now, I know how important those two qualities are—listening unconditionally and not giving stupid advice. I also know that therapists and other health care providers often fail on both of those counts.

A longtime stylist in Southern California, Michael Blomsterberg was among the first stylists to popularize this term, in fact writing a book *Hairapy: Deeper Than the Roots* (2006).[14] He is now a spiritual teacher and life coach; sitting in his salon chair gradually mutated into an experience more akin to sitting on a shrink's couch. He describes his goals to appreciate and accept his clients for who they really are and to provide a safe space for them to make changes that will transform their lives "from the automatic to the authentic." That is a far cry from a haircut or color, but with the right relationship, hairapy may deliver all of that.

The trust that often forms between clients and stylists is truly unique. Again, as a therapist myself, I know that trust must be earned—it is never just given away. I spoke to Patricia Fripp, now an award-winning inspirational speaker, coach and trainer who was a hairstylist in California for 24 years. She put it simply: "People have a unique relationship with the person that makes them beautiful. Sitting in that chair, people feel they are the only person in the universe. It's one of very few jobs where touch is appropriate, necessary and legal." She went on to say that once her clients realized she would keep everything to herself, they would tell her everything, opening up a potential level of trust that we rarely experience. Fripp was one of the first women to do men's hair. Until then it had been exclusively a male business. She enjoyed her work with men immensely, recognizing that she was one of the few people her male clients felt were safe, allowing them truly to be themselves.[15]

Without doubt, the client-stylist relationship is very special. Our stylists hold a weapon near our heads, and we let them touch us much more than we allow in most professional relationships. I call this trust on steroids. As a close friend expressed, "when people touch you, you start to talk."

Although we talk about hairapy as therapy, it really is not the same. Therapy assumes a tacit agreement that the client needs to do transformational work to improve themselves in some way that could be quite uncomfortable and upsetting. Talking openly about deep, dark secrets is transformational. Hairapy is far less challenging and more accepting of the person as is. Another difference is that usually the client and the stylist are both looking at the mirror—not eye to eye, face to face as in psychotherapy. This gives some distance and ease.

Most people love to talk about themselves to someone who listens. A priest will listen to a confession but will prescribe penance. Therapists may not prescribe penance, but we usually reflect on changes the person could make to improve things in their life or suggest ways to expand their self-awareness and insight. It might feel like penance to some of our patients.

A friend will listen but then will be watching you afterward, sometimes with judgment or commentary. But hair stylists expect nothing of clients other than that their appearance will change from the beginning to the end of the appointment. They actually expect much more of themselves as they aim to deliver the look or feeling each client seeks. Stylists need to tune into each client to figure out what will satisfy these desires and result in a happy customer. It requires more than most of us realize.

Many of the women I interviewed while writing this book described their stylist as a critically important touchstone throughout the years.

- "I would fly from my home in New England to Ohio every two months for several years. Our relationship is important. It's very trusting—I tell her things I don't tell others."
- "My hairdresser/stylist is my confidant and I have openly admitted to having a 'girl crush' on her for years. I trust her with knowing what I want or need to do with my hair, i.e., cut, trim, highlights, lowlights, etc., etc., when even I don't know what I want. I wish everyone in my life could know me so well. When I move to a new city, finding the right hairstylist is as important to me as finding the right OB-GYN. Actually, the hairstylist probably comes first."
- "I share things with her that I do not tell another soul. I feel comfortable because she is sharing about herself too. Because I trust her, I'm willing to take risks with color or style."
- "I don't have to be Frau Dr. Professor this-that-or-the-other-thing when I go to the stylist. I can just be me and crack jokes

and read stupid women's magazines and gossip. I can just be a funny person with a head of hair they can play with—it is like entertainment. I have few relationships like that."

• "It is nice to go and get taken care of and laugh. It is like therapy but without all the angst."

The Dark Side

Client-stylist interactions are not all warm and fuzzy with joyous results. According to one study, more than 20 percent of women have cried after a haircut at least once in their life, with 10 percent refusing to pay and 1 percent threatening to sue.[16] My stylist recounts stories of women fainting during haircuts, overwhelmed by the loss of control as they experience even a slightly changed hairstyle—and one that they requested.

Breaking up with a hairstylist can be a major trauma. In Chapter 12, Joan described how "my mid-life crisis happened right on top of my head." At the time, she had started to struggle with body image and some other issues triggered by turning 40. When she decided to "go blond," her longtime stylist readily complied. Joan thought she looked great until a trusted friend shared her negative feelings about it. Shocked and dismayed, she went back to the salon the next day and asked to change her hair color to red. Joan was clearly looking for something, but hair color was not the answer.

She realized that her stylist was not helping her with this search for self through hair color. Despite feeling guilty, she began considering ending that relationship. Joan confesses to having talked about saying goodbye to her stylist for three years in therapy before her therapist said to her, "I'll cut your hair for you. You are way too intelligent to still be talking about this."

Walking into a new salon a few months later, Joan felt extremely uncomfortable and vulnerable. Despite being a woman who has overcome all kinds of adverse life experiences and has accomplished a great deal both personally and professionally, this felt like "one of the scariest things in my life." She was crying as she entered the unfamiliar salon, and the new stylist looked at her and asked, "What do you need from me?" That was exactly the welcome Joan needed and is a great example of the emotional telepathy stylists so often seem to have. Granted, the tears and tentative body language gave away the story, but the kindness and empathy she felt were instantly comforting and healing.

Joan learned a great deal about herself through this breakup, including that she sometimes sacrifices too much of herself to please people and that she needs to let things go and worry less about offending others. Hair can be a good teacher for all kinds of life lessons. Since the breakup, she has enjoyed going to the hairdresser and felt much freer. For the first time, she looks at her hair as a means "to have fun on top of my head. Hair constricts us or helps us blossom." Joan is right—hair can do both of those things and she is blossoming just as her hair is, as she plays with its style, length, and color. She has also changed her stylist several times since leaving that long-term relationship. She has been able to assert herself and draw effective boundaries, instead of staying with a stylist who is not meeting her needs.

In talking about her hair experiences, Joan reminisced about going to the salon for her mother's weekly appointments as a child. She remembers the smells and the experiences clearly and fondly. To this day she dreams of sitting next to her mother again in the salon having their hair done.

When her mother was in a nursing home toward the end of her life, Joan arranged to have her mother's hair done weekly so she would still have that comfortable routine. Seeing her mother look the same despite her declining health and touching her mother's hair were great solace to both. Again, hair is a unique and deeply personal connector.

Lindsey (see Chapter 8) also struggled with a bad breakup. Earlier you read that Lindsey's hair story was very tied to her mother's hair story and their relationship. When we spoke, she realized that her difficulty setting limits with her stylist and making a change also had much to do with their mother-daughter dynamics. This is what we psychotherapists call a parallel process:

Certain relationships are in your life for a period of time, but as you grow and change, they don't fit anymore. For about 10 years, it was more and more inconvenient to see her, due to my professional travel, her limited hours, and the distance and time commuting from the suburbs into the city. I had to plan a whole day to do this, and it wasn't fun or time efficient. In a way, I was hanging onto the time in my life when I was working in the city, connected to life there, but that's no longer my base.

As I thought more about this, I realized the similarities between her and my mom—both of them talk nonstop, sometimes tangentially so I never feel relaxed around them, but I don't want to say anything to hurt them, so it was hard to make this major change. I do a lot to help them, but don't necessarily get much back. It's that residual guilt about moving on and focusing more on myself. Plus, I had this fear that someone else would ruin my hair—literally that it would all fall out. She has been an important part of my support system, kept me looking my best, but somehow I know there's a primitive feeling underlying this—someone working on your head makes you vulnerable, probably like what people feel about therapists.

But I did make the change finally and I am happy about this—I feel more myself. The new stylist changed my hair a bit, gave me the products to keep it going but kept it low-maintenance and changed the color—it looks more natural. I am who I am now. I am turning 55 and the new look feels more flattering. Staying with my old stylist kept me looking the same—now I have something that I would call the old-meets-the-new-Lindsey.

Lindsey needed to face many issues when she decided to leave her stylist—and one was her unconscious desire to keep her life the same by keeping her hair and its upkeep the same. It was time to move on, to recognize that her life had changed in major ways, as she was no longer living and working in an urban environment that had been exciting and engaging but also draining. Her hair had been a way to hang onto her past instead of embracing her present and moving toward her future. Our hair stories are best when they are moving us forward and encouraging our growth and development instead of allowing us to be stagnant. Obviously, they can do either.

Till Death Do We Part

When do we make peace with our hair and no longer need the technical assistance and spiritual guidance that stylists provide? That may not happen until death or sometimes not until the funeral.

163

In preparing a body for a wake or a viewing, morticians need to pay close attention to the appearance and grooming of their deceased clients and do their best to make the dead person look as they did when alive. When done well, this sensitive service provides critical comfort and closure to the family and loved ones. This task is more challenging if the death is traumatic or disfiguring but important in all cases.

While traditional mortuaries have done all the preparation and embalming themselves, today some hire a mortuary cosmetologist for hair and makeup. Mortuary cosmetology, also known as desairology,[17] has emerged since the late 1970s and early 1980s as both the cosmetology and the mortuary industries recognized the importance of appearance in our final farewells to loved ones. Families want the deceased to look not only familiar but their very best. Especially if grooming and fashion had been a central concern, they insist that their loved one leave this earth still maintaining that standard.

I first thought about hair care for the dead after reading about a Baltimore barber who has been asked to do the hair of many young men cut down by gun violence in that city. Antoine Dow owns a barber shop in Druid Heights in West Baltimore. On a normal Saturday, he can cut the hair of as many as 70 men.[18]

Long concerned about the violence of his native city, Antoine feels a strong calling to provide a decent haircut to these young men, some of whom were his clients when they were alive. He himself was shot in the leg when he tried to intervene in an argument involving a customer who ended up dying later in the day from his gunshot. He has worked hard to create an oasis of safety for men—especially young men in his barber shop—and wants them to have the dignity we all deserve in death. He sometimes brings locks of hair from haircuts in his shop to provide covering for gunshot wounds to the head.

The connection between a hairstylist or barber and a client can be a long-lasting gift. I'm grateful to have had that experience with my stylist. Our relationship has lasted longer than most marriages!

Who Are These People?

Antoine Dow is one example of the incredible generosity of spirit and desire to help the community that we see so frequently in hair professionals. They are not only remarkably creative and caring, but they also often go the extra mile—or more—to raise money for a charity or to get attention for a deserving cause. In Antoine's case, the cause is the lives lost on the streets of Baltimore to unnecessary gun violence. Salons devoted to women are very likely to focus on breast cancer as it affects so many.

I have interviewed some remarkable stylists on my journey to write this book. One unusual and inspiring example is Deborah Rodriguez, who came from a family of hairdressers and remembers being in her mother's shop from the time she was five years old. She did not want to be in the hair business initially, feeling it was "too easy," as she already knew the job having spent all those formative years in the shop. After pursuing other career paths, she revisited the idea of a career in hair. Gradually she realized she was "a different kind of smart" and she would likely be both challenged and very satisfied working with hair.[19]

Since then, she not only has success as a stylist, as a business-woman and as an author, but she has started a beauty school in Afghanistan to help women gain financial independence and positive self-esteem. Her book *Kabul Beauty School: An American Woman Goes Behind the Veil*[20] describes her adventure. She arrived in Kabul as part of a humanitarian mission during a period of transition in her personal life. Responding to the intense interest her career as a hair stylist evoked from the women she met, Rodriguez helped to create a beauty school in Kabul. She recognized that helping these women to develop skills, self-confidence, and even financial independence might enhance their individual lives as well as promote healing of their postwar country. Her book chronicles the key role a beauty school or salon can have in a woman's life and in a community as so many salons across the globe do. Since the collapse of Afghanistan in the late summer of 2021, after the American troop withdrawal, it is unclear what has happened to the beauty school, its successful graduates, and its current students. The beauty school did graduate more than 200 women, launching them into greater economic stability and even autonomy, but that may now have dissipated due to the current political powers and attitudes toward women's place in society. Still, what Deborah Rodriguez contributed to the women and the community by creating a beauty school is inspiring.

Around Every Corner

Hair salons seem to be around every corner—they are one of the things I look for when visiting a new town or city. I think of hair salons and barber shops as the heartbeats of their communities due to an impressive altruism and deep desire to contribute to the lives of others. Probably in every community in the United States, hair salons sponsor programs like my town's annual haircut-a-thon. Once a year, a local salon devotes a Sunday to this, with all proceeds (now hundreds of thousands of dollars!) going to support breast cancer research at our local medical center.

Some salons go even further. In 2003, Racine's Spa and Salon in Islip, New York, started a non-profit foundation called Mondays at Racine to help women maintain a sense of control as they face cancer.[21] Two sisters, Cynthia and Rachel, had seen what cancer did to their mother. For many women, the impact of the cancer and the treatment is not only frightening and painful, but it also changes their appearance and their relationship with their bodies. Cynthia and Rachel realized women often no longer feel beautiful and become reclusive and even depressed, especially if they live in a community where the beauty ideal is very strong. Having opened their hearts and their heads to the impact of cancer on a woman's sense of self and mood, they decided to open their salon as well.

Since starting this program, Racine's has been open on Mondays only to cancer patients, providing them the opportunity to deal with the emotions of their illness in solidarity with others on similar journeys and to have massages and facials, haircuts and colors, and any other treatment offered by the salon. The simple philosophy is that when a woman is going through cancer treatment, she needs a day of beauty because she does not feel one bit beautiful. Its mission is "to reduce the physical, emotional and cosmetic side effects of chemotherapy and radiation by providing free in the salon beauty and wellness services." Racine's has expanded to include both men and women undergoing chemotherapy and radiation.

Racine's now has a charter program where it helps other salons to transplant this model. In my community, inspired by Racine's story, Cut Out Cancer @ Milano is open two Mondays a month to cancer patients and provides a range of beauty services and other treatments like massage, reiki, and art therapy.[22] Its mantra "treat the person, not the cancer" is a welcome reminder to women that they are still the women they were before their illness.

The nonprofit organization Wigs & Wishes has a network of hairstylists and salon owners making a significant difference in the lives of women and children as they battle cancer throughout the world. Founded by Martino Cartier, a hair stylist and inspirational speaker based in New Jersey, and supported by individual donations, corporate sponsors and fundraising events, its premise is simply "if you look good, you will feel good." Through Wigs & Wishes, salons and stylists provide wigs and complimentary services to women, hoping to give them support, confidence and strength to face their illness. It also fulfills wishes that children express as they go through the treatment process. Wigs & Wishes' website has many smiling faces and stories of renewal and hope. Since 2012, it has donated more than 100,000 wigs.[23]

Cut It Out

Another example of the remarkable good that stylists and salons do—too often with little if any recognition—is the Cut It Out program run by the Professional Beauty Association.[24] Originating in Birmingham in 2004, Cut It Out capitalizes on the trusting relationship women have with their stylists, with the goal of identifying and ending domestic violence. Cut It Out has trained stylists all over the country about the signs of domestic violence using a PowerPoint presentation on myths and facts about domestic violence and teaching ways to approach the subject with a client, including contact information for the National Domestic Violence Hotline as well as local crisis services.

Through its "Give the Power Back" initiative, Cut It Out encourages beauty professionals, students, and salons to help their local domestic violence agencies to get this problem out of the darkness and into the light where women can be helped. With the statement "domestic violence stops at the chair," Cut It Out empowers stylists to not only recognize the signs of domestic violence but also to empower victims and help them to get to a safer place in their lives. Providing educational materials to salons creates settings where clients are likely to feel safe and to disclose the secrets of their lives when they are ready.

The beauty salon may be one of the very few places a victim of domestic violence goes by herself. There she is likely to have close, and sometimes even exclusive, attention of a caring human being who may notice emotional or physical signs of abuse like depression, bruises, or bald spots where hair has been pulled or has fallen out due to stress. Even women who are on top of their health maintenance usually only see their PCP once a year and dentist twice a year. In contrast, they are likely to see their stylist multiple times a year. Over those visits, trust builds, and women may be more receptive to their stylist's input and observations than to any others. They also may feel less judged by their stylist than they do by their physician or other care providers.

The hair industry is full of amazing altruism and deep commitment to their clientele and their communities. If only we could clone such positive energy and disseminate it throughout the world. Once more, we see that hair is never just hair. It always tells an important story.

Far from a cosmetic concern, hair is about connection, to the self, to others, and to the world around us. The people who travel with us on our hair journeys are truly essential workers. They often bring out the best in us—not just the best of our hair, but of our true selves. I thank all of them!

Conclusion:
Connection, Connection, Connection

"It's remarkable and humbling to realize that, in the final analysis, the only certain thing we know about hair is that, however it is styled and whatever shape it takes, it always means something to every person who sees it, though few of us may agree on what that something is."—Scott Lowe[1]

Hair is all about connection—to the past, to our race or ethnicity or religion, to our families, to our cultural zeitgeist, to our friends and partners, and to ourselves. The top of our heads may truly be the doorway to our souls and to our most rewarding and meaningful relationships. Hair matters.

It seems only right that *Hair Tells a Story* concludes with some unique examples of the relational power of hair. Enjoy these as your own understanding of the relational nature of your hair evolves.

What's Your Hair Secret?

My final request when interviewing women was "Tell me a secret no one else knows about you and your hair." Not everyone had a secret to share but the story below has continued to move me. I think about it frequently, as it speaks to the profoundly personal meaning hair can have and the deep connection with others it can symbolize.

Tara spoke directly and powerfully about experiencing her beloved brother's sudden death 30 years earlier. His death was tragic and unexpected—a shock to her and to their family and friends and community. She remembered being at the wake the evening before the funeral, aware of her own deep disconnection and disbelief as countless people filed through the traditional mourning process. She felt ungrounded and uncertain as she considered living her life without him. At the end of the wake, she asked her parents and the funeral director if she could have some time alone with her brother. She was lost and confused about how to say goodbye to him. She describes:

> It was then that I decided that I needed somehow to keep a piece of him. I looked at his tie, the handkerchief in his suit pocket. I needed something but none of this seemed "right." Then I figured it out ... a piece of him ... his hair.... His dark hair framed his angular face beautifully. His dark brown eyes and his smile, in between those locks, drew you in, captured you. Such kindness ... such warmth. How to live without that? I looked around the viewing room for a knife or scissors. Nothing. I looked around again. The wooden double doors leading to the hall remained closed. We were alone. I leaned over and bit a lock of my brother's hair. I tucked it into my wallet and carried it with me for years.

She kept that secret for decades, until sharing it with me. A locket of his hair kept Tara upright and able to walk through her overwhelming grief. Touching his hair and knowing she had it nearby allowed her to fulfill her desperately desired ongoing connection with him.

Hair can keep us close emotionally even if we have never been conscious of this desire until a moment like Tara experienced. She needed her brother to still be in her life and a tuft of his hair was the only thing that could provide that connection especially in the early days after his death.

How do you feel about Tara's secret?

Do you have a secret? Take some time to figure out its meaning if you do.

A Favorite Memory

After talking with me about my perspectives on what hair can represent, a close friend shared this memory with me. Molly has been an ally on the journey of helping women to live their best lives and escape all the body shaming our culture teaches them. I always learn from her. For context, Molly was the fourth of six sisters in her Irish family.

> One of my favorite memories is with my older sister (#2) taking me (#4) on the back of her bicycle up to the avenue to the "European Hair Salon," where Mrs. S., our next-door neighbor and first-generation Italian immigrant, operated her own beauty salon. I had this idea that she would make me sophisticated like I imagined European girls to be. That's exactly what my sister promised and what I really, really wanted.
>
> Instead, each time we went, Mrs. S. would look at me and then run her hands through my wavy red hair while repeating in her heavy accent, "Layers will bring out the curl" and "Look now at the curls." I looked each time and each time I thought I was lucky to have curls, but I hated my red hair. I didn't look like the European girl I so wanted to be. My sister would smile and thank her, leaving cash and a tip on the table as we left. I would climb up on the backseat of her bicycle and away we would go, with me a little heartbroken, returning home to my mother who would exclaim, "Yes, that looks much better."
>
> Years went by and I became increasingly jealous of my sisters #1, 2, 3, 5, and 6. They were all blessed with straight blond and brunette hair like Cher and other famous girls on TV—like the Mod Squad teens. I wanted so badly to look like that too. Instead, people called me "Carrot Top" or "Red."
>
> Whenever I was bullied like that, I would explode into temper tantrums to express my rage. I felt so different and wanted to fade into the crowd but couldn't with this hair. In time, I learned to accept that I was the first born "red head" and named after my mother in her liking. It took years, but as I got a bit older, I got to the point of feeling blessed to have my hair!
>
> I find it odd that this hair story is now one of my very favorite memories, and a reminder of special childhood experiences, when my hair had been a source of pain for so long.

Molly had desperately wanted to be like her sisters and other role models—the "European girls" and the media icons. Her beautiful red hair set her apart but has since become a source of pride and connection to her Irish heritage and to her mother.

Has your hair ever been a source of disconnection or shame as Molly's was?

"My hair is what starts conversations"

For Syd, hair has been a connecting factor her entire life. Growing up, she had long blond hair. Now interspersed with lighter and whiter hair, it still looks blond—that is, with help from her stylist. Whenever she goes to reunions or events back in her hometown, her hair instantly identifies her and creates connection. Often, people she has not seen in years—or even decades—will call out her name, just because of those distinctive locks:

> My hair is what starts conversations. They always seem to be in awe of how "exactly the same" I look. For me, this has subtly translated into a few potent metamessages—like it's a *good* thing that I haven't changed (as long as it's my hair and it was OK to start with) and I must somehow be the same *person*. I know they mean this as a compliment and that my hair is almost a cherished form of connection, but I also experience it as pressure, like I need to keep it looking this way so we can maintain our youth—and our relationships.

On a trip to Europe in middle school, Syd remembers how much attention her hair attracted from boys and men—this was unsettling. It was not starting conversations then, but it did start contact— sometimes unwanted and usually confusing. Syd had always been a "tomboy" and never experienced anything like this.

> If I stood still, in the store, on the sidewalk, and especially on the subway, men of all ages played with my hair. It was simultaneously frightening and intoxicating. No one had ever related to me in that way—especially boys, who were still my primary playmates. As a tomboy, I was clueless about what to do with this objectification process. They'd smile, ogle, laugh, and my friends and our group leader would find it entertaining. I was mystified at first, but it awakened my experience of my femininity.
>
> I wasn't uncomfortable with my tomboy tendencies. I actually had pride about my ability to hold my own with the boys on the block, but I had seen them starting to pay attention to other girls. I wasn't sure where I fit in this changing landscape. In contrast to my experience at home, these guys were relating to me decidedly as a female. Their fascination with my long blond hair ignited my awareness of my gender identity and sexual orientation—it helped me realize I was female, and I was beginning to feel attraction to boys. From that moment forward, my hair became the essence of my femininity.

Syd is now in her late 50s and her hair continues to be a key ingredient in her body image and personal identity. Growing up in a male-dominated family, she has always loved sports and is more athletic than most women—in fact, more than many men as well. That long blond hair has come to validate her sexuality and to allow Syd to feel accepted by both the male and the female subcultures in which she is immersed.

Our talk stimulated profound memories about how her family related to hair as well. Both parents had beautiful hair, were impeccably groomed, and devoted to their stylists. Her mother had serious psychiatric issues, but her hair always looked perfect, with her longtime, loyal stylist coming to their home on the days her depression kept her from venturing to the salon. And her father was also nearly ritualistic in his hair care—monthly appointments with his stylist were non-negotiable despite a very busy professional schedule. Her brothers followed suit. As she described her current hair care, Syd has clearly developed a similar relationship with her stylist—she depends on her and makes no hair decisions on her own. With both her stylist and her husband expressing such great love for her hair, she is unlikely to ever have it cut.

Hair is a safe spot, like a sanctuary, and something Syd always feels good about. Although she admits that she tends to negate compliments that come her way, she can readily accept them if they concern her hair.

For Syd, hair not only starts conversations but also creates and continues connections, with others and with herself. She is still discovering its impact on her personal identity and her life trajectory.

What role has your hair played in your emerging identity and sexuality?

How has hair figured into your family dynamics and behavior patterns? What importance did it have?

* * *

Once more, these stories reveal the relational relevance of hair. Once more, we can say with certainty, "Hair tells a story."

Hair matters. It matters personally, socially, sexually, spiritually, culturally, ethnically, globally. Since the beginning of time, hair has served as a second language, telling the story of women's lives like nothing else does. I hope this journey through the story of hair has enhanced your connections to yourself, your history, your relationships, and your passions. Happy trails to you! And happy hair!

Appendix:
Questions and Exercises

"And forget not that the earth delights to feel your bare feet and the winds long to play with your hair."—Kahlil Gibran[1]

Hair-Raising Questions and Experiential Exercises

Before starting to consider these questions or do the experiential exercises, take a minute to pause and open up to your inner experience. Utilize your beginner's mind.[2] Approach this process with an open mind and heart, a desire for discovery, and no preconceived answers. Beginner's mind is a way of staying in the present, the way young children experience the world, without expectations and a script predicting what is coming next. It is much more fun than believing you have all the answers. Try it.

Narrating Your Hair Story

Consider writing the narrative of your hair as I did in *Hair and Me* (Chapter 7). Here are questions that may provoke some thoughts. Thinking about these questions alone will evoke insights, memories, and connections. Writing will help to crystalize their meaning, but these would also be positive things to talk about with friends or in a small group.

Remember that a story is a living thing. It will change over time, and it should never be rushed. Feel no pressure if your story is slow to come to you. It will be worth the wait.

What does your hair mean to you?

Did hair have any special meaning in your family?

Imagine the day you were born. What do you think people said about your hair? What do you wish they had said?

Was your hair similar to your mother's? Father's? Other family members'?

Have there been times that you felt your hair belonged to someone else (family, boyfriend, husband, partner, etc.) and not to you?

What emotions come to mind most often when you think about your hair?

Has your hair changed over time? Any pattern to that?

Have you ever used your hair to signal a major shift in your life or in your psyche?

If the narrative for your hair changed, would your life change?

What do you want more of in your life? What do you want less of? How might changing your hairstyle help that to happen?

Do you let others touch your hair? What does it mean to you when people do touch your hair?

Did you ever have a slumber party when you fussed with each other's hair? What was that like?

Any traumatic events with hair?

Describe your favorite memory related to your hair.

What do you wish your hair looked like? Draw it, describe it or find a picture of it.

Find old photos from earlier stages in your life. What is your hair saying in these?

What role does your hair play in your body self?

Has your hair expressed personal, social, or political messages for you?

Has your hair ever been part of a battle for autonomy?

What does the word hair evoke for you? What does it mean?

Rapunzel's hair attracted a prince who climbed up to her in her stairless parlor. What connections do you make between hair and romance? Have you seen it as a way to "catch a man" or attract a partner?

What meaning do you ascribe to other people's hair? Jealousy? Envy? Desire? Disgust?

Do you draw a lot of conclusions or make judgments based on hair?

Describe a time that you were right and another when you were wrong.

Do you consider stylists essential workers?

What do you feel about your stylist? Have you ever told him or her?

What's your favorite memory of a salon or hair experience?

If you were designing the ideal prototype of the salon or barbershop of the future, what would it be like?

What would your ideal hair experience be like?

Experiential Exercises

WIG PARTY

Get a group of fun women together and have some refreshments and music going as you gather for the afternoon or evening. (Alternatively, you could do this alone, but be sure to talk about it with someone so you can learn more from the experience.)

Invest in a few inexpensive wigs and ask friends to bring any wigs they have as well. Have all the wigs on a table—enough for the number of guests and a couple of extras if possible. Have mirrors around so people can see themselves—a combination of hand mirrors and wall mirrors is best but not essential. Also have a small pad and pen available for each guest so she can write about the experience.

Ask that each grab a wig, put it on, and circulate—talking, dancing, laughing, having fun.

Have a timer go off every 10 to 15 minutes. At that point, the party stops, and each guest writes a little about what it was like to wear that wig. You can also talk together about your experience. Repeat this for four or five cycles.

Then take turns describing the whole experience. Which was your favorite wig? Least favorite? How did the wigs affect you? Did you feel like a different person or still feel like yourself? Any surprises?

Next decide which wig you'd like to wear for the rest of the evening. If more than one guest wants the same wig, talk about it and work it out.

Continue to have fun and enjoy each other and your fake hair. Compare how you feel with your own natural hair versus how you felt with the wigs. Did the wigs bring out different aspects of your personality? Do you want to make any changes in your life or with your hair based on this experience?

CLUSTERING

Clustering, or "Rico clustering," named after its creator Gabriele Rico, is a brainstorming tool that can be used as a writing tool, a teaching tool, a therapy tool, or just as a way to free up our thinking about a subject and get to a deeper meaning. It bridges the openness and connection-making of the left-brain with the verbalization and ordering of the right-brain and helps us to get "unstuck." Then we can make connections and think more spontaneously. It allows you to have fewer filters and critiques of your thinking and can be used for many activities.

This task is simplified and adapted from Gabriele Rico's "Clustering Task."[3] It can be done alone or in a group.

To begin you will need a piece of blank paper and pencil or pen.

1. Draw a circle on the page and write the word "HAIR" in the circle.

2. Draw six to eight straight lines, like sunrays, coming from the circle.

3. Without thinking, write on each line the very first word that comes to mind. Work rapidly and let it flow—without censoring.

4. With all lines now full, come back to an empty space on the paper and begin to write a sentence, story or poem using the words and any other associations you wish.

5. Share your words with someone important to you or frame your paper to remind you of what you learned.

You can use this exercise with other aspects of identity or body image—again, it is best if you share the experience so you can learn more and get support or validation.

THE SOCIAL GATHERING

This experiential task adapted from Adrienne Ressler's "Social Party"[4] exercise is intended to help us grasp how the attitudes of others toward us and our hair shape our identity.

Part I

1. Four to five willing participants come together in an imagined social gathering.

2. Each person is asked to find a word that someone influential has used to describe their hair which offends them somehow, for example, "wild," "blondie," "thick," "ugly," "flat."

3. Members of the group walk around and greet others with a handshake and an introduction such as "Hi, I am wild," "I am blondie," "I am thick," "I am ugly," "I am flat."

4. Following the introductions to all other guests, each individual pauses and shares what that experience felt like and what it evokes. What memories or emotions were stirred up by this experience?

Part II

5. Next the participants pause and contemplate a positive word or description about their hair—something another has said or one's own feeling, like "easy," "colorful," "attractive," "gorgeous," etc.

6. Again each person uses that word as an introduction to others: "I am easy," "I am colorful," "I am attractive," "I am gorgeous," etc.

7. Following the exchange, each individual pauses and shares what it felt like and how it differed from the earlier exchange.

Take some time to reflect on your usual self-talk about your hair—is it negative, as in Part I, positive, as in Part II, or mixed?

How about finding the positive aspects of your hair and emphasizing those in your self-talk?

Share these insights.

Chapter Notes

Introduction

1. Alinejad, M. (2018). *The wind in my hair*. Little, Brown, p. 30.
2. Moorhead, J. (2018, June 2). The wind in my hair: One Iranian woman's courageous struggle against being forced to wear the hijab. *The Guardian.* https://www.theguardian.com/global/2018/jun/03/the.

Chapter 1

1. McCracken, G. (1995). *Big hair: A journey into the transformation of self.* The Overlook Press, p. 2.
2. Scheper-Hughes, N., & Lock, M. (1987). The mindful body: A prolegomenon to future work in medical anthropology. *Medical Anthropology Quarterly* 1: 6–41.
3. Trasko, M. (1994). *Daring do's: A history of extraordinary hair.* Flammarion, p. 29.
4. Sherrow, V. (2006). *Encyclopedia of hair: A cultural history.* Greenwood Press, pp. 242–43.
5. Trasko 1994.
6. Sherrow 2006.
7. Lowe, S. (2016). *Object lessons: Hair.* Bloomsbury Academic.
8. Johnstone, P.L.W. (2013, Aug. 11). Elders talk about significance of long hair in Native American cultures. www.whitewolfpack.com/2013/08/.html.
9. https://www.goodreads.com/author/quotes/3004479.Coco_Chanel.

Chapter 2

1. Mahdawhi, A. (2014, Jan. 10). Hair is the western woman's veil. *The Guardian.* https://www.theguardian.com/commentisfree/2014/jan/10/hair-western-woman-veil-femininity.
2. Kreamer, A. (2007). *Going gray: How to embrace your authentic self with grace and style.* Little, Brown.
3. Garcia, I. (2017, May 24). Studies prove the link between hair & confidence. *Naturally Curly.* https://www.naturallycurly.com/curlreading/seniors/.
4. The psychology of hair. (2011, Aug. 8). https://www.youbeauty.com/beauty/psychology-of-hair.
5. Wood, H. (2019, Sept. 21). 27 Hair color statistics, facts & industry trends (that will blow your mind). https://www.holleewoodhair.com/hair-color-statistics.
6. The psychology of hair 2011.
7. Bennett, J. (2009, Mar. 29). Are we turning tweens into generation diva? *Newsweek.* https://www.newsweek.com/are-we-turning-tweens-generation-diva-76425.
8. Escobar, S. (2018, Oct. 15). How young is too young to dye your kid's hair? That patch test is more important now than ever. *Good Housekeeping.* https://www.goodhousekeeping.com/beauty/hair/a38165/how-young-is-too-young-to-color.
9. Sonmez, F. (2010, June 13). No apology from Fiorina for comment on Boxer's hairstyle. *Washington Post.* voices.washingtonpost.com/44/2010/06/no-apology-from-fiorina-on-box.html.
10. Zernike, K. (2001, May 21). Commencements: At Yale, Mrs. Clinton ponders hair and politics. *New York Times.* https://www.nytimes.com/2001/05/21/

181

nyregion/commencements-at-yale-mrs-clinton-ponders-hair-and-politics.html.
11. Marty, R. (2016, Apr. 27). 7 things women in politics could never get away with (but men can). *Cosmopolitan*. www.cosmopolitan.com/politics/news/.../female-male-politicians-double-standards/.
12. Wheeler, R.B., & Everyday Health. (2016, Aug. 12). Is a bad hair day bad for your health? *The Mercury News*. https://www.mercurynews.com/2013/02/06/is-a-bad-hair-day-bad-for-your-health.

Chapter 3

1. Simon, D. (2000). *Hair: Public, political, extremely personal*. Thomas Dunne, p. 171.
2. Jung, C.G. (2009). *The red book*. W.W. Norton.
3. Jung, C.G., and Douglas, C. (Ed.). (1997). *Visions: Notes of the seminar given in 1930–1934*, Volume 1. Princeton University Press.
4. *Ibid.*
5. *Ibid.*
6. Sherrow 2006.
7. Lowe 2016.
8. Stenn, K. (2016). *Hair: A human history*. Pegasus.
9. Etcoff, N. (2000). *Survival of the prettiest: The science of beauty*. Anchor.
10. Trasko 1994.
11. Sherrow 2006, xxi.
12. Levine, M.M. (1995). The gendered grammar of ancient Mediterranean hair. In Eliberg-Schwartz, H., & Doniger, W. (Eds.), *Off with her head! The denial of women's identity in myth, religion and culture*. University of California Press, pp. 76–130.
13. Sherrow 2006, p. 261.
14. University Archives. (2022, Jan. 6). Our founder: John Reznikoff. https://www.universityarchives.com/pages/john-reznikoff.
15. Chopra, D. (1993). *Ageless body, timeless mind*. Harmony.
16. Sherrow 2006, p. 144.
17. Lowe 2016.
18. Stenn 2016.
19. Sullivan, L., & Deslauriers, L.

(2016). *Awakening hair: Caring for your cosmic antenna*. Sundream.
20. Sherrow 2006.
21. Lowe 2016.
22. www.songlyrics.com/hair/hair-lyrics.
23. https://www.youtube.com/watch?v=wldi5fADGmc.
24. https://genius.com/Lady-gaga-hair-lyrics.

Chapter 4

1. Charlton, E. (2012, Nov. 11). Age-old story of hair. *The Star Malaysia*. https://www.pressreader.com/malaysia/the-star-malaysia-star2/20121111/281801396233282.
2. Sherrow 2006, p. xx.
3. *Ibid.*, pp. 12–13.
4. Byrd, A.D., & Tharps, L. (2002). *Hair story: Untangling the roots of black hair in America*. St. Martin's.
5. 'Okhai Ojeikere, J.D. (2000). *Photographs*. Scalo.
6. Byrd & Tharps 2002.
7. Lowe 2016, p. 124.
8. Budge, E.W. (2003). *From fetish to god in Ancient Egypt*. Kessinger, p. 89.
9. Stenn 2016.
10. Sherrow 2006.
11. Trasko 1994.
12. Brownmiller, S. (1984). *Femininity*. Fawcett Columbine.
13. Trasko 1994.
14. *Ibid.*
15. *Ibid.*
16. Gill, N.S. (2019, Apr. 4). The great poet Ovid: Publius Ovidius Naso (43 BCE–CE 17). https://www.thoughtco.com/ovid-overview-of-the-latin-poet-112463.
17. Ovid. (1982). *The erotic poems*. Trans. Peter Green. Penguin, p. 218.
18. Trasko 1994.
19. Sherrow 2006.
20. Williams, S. (2016, Aug. 4). A village of Rapunzels! Inside the ancient community where women only cut their hair ONCE in their lives. *Daily Mail*. https://www.dailymail.co.uk/news/peoplesdaily/article-3723244/A-village-Rapunzels-Inside-ancient-community-women-cut-hair-lives.html.

21. Hair today, gone tomorrow. (2012, Sept. 20). https://www.iol.co.za/travel/world/europe/hair-today-gone-tomorrow-1387529. Retrieved 13 Jan. 2022.

22. St. Baldrick's Foundation | Childhood Cancer Research Charity. https://www.stbaldricks.org. Retrieved 13 Jan. 2022.

23. Tarlo, E. (2016). *Entanglement: The secret lives of hair.* One World.

24. Cherished hair: Frivolities and trophies. Cheveux Cheris. Musée du quai Branly—Jacques Chirac—Cheveux chéris. https://www.quaibranly.fr › cheveux-cheris-34701. Retrieved 15 Jan. 2022.

25. Brownmiller 1984.

26. Bestselling barbie doll. https://www.guinnessworldrecords.com/world-records/best-selling-barbie-doll. Retrieved 13 Jan. 2021.

27. Alcott, L.M. (1989). *Little women.* Penguin Classics.

28. Henry, O. (1906). The gift of the Magi. *The four million.* CreateSpace Independent Publishing Platform (24 May 2017).

29. Fitzgerald, F.S. (2009). *Bernice bobs her hair and other stories.* Dover.

Chapter 5

1. Tannen, D. (2015). Why mothers and daughters tangle over hair. In E. Benedict (ed.), *Me, my hair, and I: 27 women untangle an obsession.* Algonquin Books of Chapel Hill, p. 109.

2. *Ibid.*

3. Rhode, D. (2010). *The beauty bias: The injustice of appearance in life and law.* Oxford University Press.

4. Rhode, D. (2014, Mar. 13). Personal communication.

5. Luo, M., & Horyn, C. (2008, Dec. 5). 3 Palin stylists cost campaign more than $165,000. *New York Times.* https://www.nytimes.com/2008/12/06/us/politics/06palin.html.

6. Trasko 1994.

7. Smith, D. (2010, Nov. 26). Personal communication.

8. Verastegui, A.C. (2021, July 29). Female athletes battling gender bias in Tokyo 2021. https://redshoemovement.com/female-athletes-battling-gender-bias-in-tokyo-2021.

9. Young, J.Y. (2021, Aug. 30). She just won her third gold medal in Tokyo. Detractors in South Korea are criticizing her haircut. *New York Times.* https://www.nytimes.com/2021/07/30/sports/olympics/an-san-hair.html.

10. www.britannica.com/topic/Lorelei-German-legend Lorelei | Definition, Story, & Facts | Britannica. Retrieved 3 Dec. 2021.

11. Trasko 1994.

12. https://www.biblegateway.com/passage/?search=1+Corinthians+11%3A14-15&version=NIV. Retrieved 3 Dec. 2021.

13. Brownmiller 1984, p. 60.

14. Sherrow 2006, p. 242.

15. Levine 1995.

16. Baskin, J.R. (2008). Jewish practices & rituals: Covering of the head. http://www.jewishvirtuallibrary.org/covering-of-the-head.

17. Sherrow 2006.

18. Trasko 1994.

19. Delaney, C. (1995). Untangling the meanings of hair in Turkish society. In H. Eliberg-Schwartz & W. Doniger (eds.), *Off with her head! The denial of women's identity in myth, religion and culture.* University of California Press, pp. 53–75.

20. Linder, D.O. (2017). The trial of Joan of Arc: An account. http://law2.umkc.edu › faculty › projects › ftrials › joan.

21. Stenn 2016.

22. Sherrow 2006, p. 288.

23. Simon 2000.

24. Brownmiller 1984, p. 67.

25. Simon 2000.

26. Sherrow 2006.

27. Brownmiller 1984.

28. Trasko 1994, p. 113.

29. Antoine. (1946). *Antoine by Antoine.* W.H. Allen.

30. Pergament, P. (1999, Dec. 4). It's not just hair: Historical and cultural considerations for an emerging technology. Symposium on Legal Disputes Over Body Tissue 75.1. https://www.scribd.com/

document/330748948/Its-Not. Retrieved 3 Dec. 2021.

31. Nightspot with racially discriminatory policy settles case with DOJ: ACLU Lawsuit Pending. (2008, Feb. 12). https://www.aclu.org/press-releases/nightspot-racially-discriminatory-policy-settles-case-doj-aclu-lawsuit-pending?redirect=racial-justice/nightspot-racially-discriminatory-

Chapter 6

1. Complete Works of Edith Wharton, https://whartoncompleteworks.org/about. Retrieved 3 Dec. 2021.

2. American Association of University Women. (n.d.). The simple truth about the gender pay gap. https://www.aauw.org/resources/article/fast-facts-pay-gap/. Retrieved 3 Dec. 2021.

3. Akhtar, A., & Baer, D. (2019, Oct. 8). 11 scientific reasons why attractive people are more successful in life. *Business Insider.* https://www.businessinsider.com/beautiful-people-make-more-money-2014-11.

4. Lowe 2016, p. 124.

5. Ferguson, S. (2017, June 23). How expensive is your hair? *Daily Mail.* https://www.dailymail.co.uk/femail/article-4633248/How-Money-Women-America-Spend-Hair.html.

6. Ephron, N. (2006). *I feel bad about my neck: And other thoughts on being a woman.* Vintage, p. 34.

7. Sickler, J. (2021, July 15). Beauty industry: cosmetic market share, trends, and statistics. https://terakeet.com/blog/beauty-industry/.

8. Hair and scalp care market size report, 2021–2028 (grandviewresearch.com). Nov. 2021.

9. Hardach, S. (2008, Feb. 18). Japanese women hairstyles track economy ups and downs. Reuters. https://www.reuters.com/article/us-japan-hair-idUST33173720080218. Retrieved 3 Dec. 2021.

10. Wilson, J. (2013, Aug. 15). Oprah's Afro wig on O Magazine's September 2013 cover is totally awesome. *Huffington Post.* www.huffpost.com/entry/oprah-

afro-wig-o-magazine-september-2013_n_3709243.

11. Brownmiller 1984.

12. https://www.oprah.com › style › Oprahs-Wig-O-Magazi... O Magazine (hair issue). (2013, Sept.). Retrieved 3 Dec. 2021.

13. *Good Hair.* (2009, Sept. 30). http://www.oprah.com/entertainment/Chris-Rocks-Good-Hair-Documentary/3#ixzz2TZcx5EY4. Retrieved 3 Dec. 2021.

14. Wilson, C. (2020, June 5). The top 50 black owned haircare brands you should know. https://www.naturallycurly.com/curlreading/curls/the-top-50-black-owned-hair-care-brands.

15. Sherrow 2006.

16. Byron, E. (2010, June 30). When a bad hair day brings you down. *Wall Street Journal.* https://www.wsj.com/articles/BL-JB-10672 When a Bad Hair Day Brings You Down.

17. Pantene introduces Priyanka Chopra as newest global ambassador. (2016, Dec. 20). *Business Wire.* https://www.businesswire.com/news/home/20161220005522/en/Pantene-Introduces-Priyanka-Chopra-as-Newest-Global-Ambassador. Retrieved 3 Dec. 2021.

Chapter 7

1. Benedict, E. (2015). *Me, my hair, and I: 27 women untangle an obsession.* Algonquin Books of Chapel Hill, p. xiii.

2. Engeln, R. (2017). *Beauty sick: How the cultural obsession with appearance hurts girls and women.* Harper.

Chapter 8

1. Tannen 2015, p. 114.

2. Benedict 2015.

3. Tannen, D. (2006). *You're wearing that? Understanding mothers and daughters in conversation.* Random House, p. 34.

4. Tannen 2015.

5. Ephron 2006, p. 32.

6. Bateson, M. (1994). *With a daugh-*

ter's eye: A memoir of Margaret Mead and Gregory Bateson. Harper Perennial.

Chapter 9

1. *Good hair.* (2009). Maya Angelou as self—IMDb. https://www.imdb.com/title/tt1213585/characters/nm0029723. Retrieved 14 Jan. 2021.
2. Sawyer, D. (n.d.). 45 Quotes by Diane Sawyer (page 2). https://www.azquotes.com/author/13038-Diane_Sawyer?p=2. Retrieved 14 Jan. 2021.

Chapter 10

1. Simon 2000, p. 171.
2. Clarendon, D. (2018, May 13). You'll never see Dolly Parton's real hair—She doesn't leave the house without a wig! *Closer Weekly.* www.closerweekly.com › posts › dolly-parton-real-hair-159778.
3. Office of Public Affairs, University of Utah. (2018, Feb. 2). Splitting the hairs of balding and hair loss. https://healthcare.utah.edu/healthfeed/postings/2018/02/hair-loss.php.
4. Harvard Health Publishing. (2020, Aug. 31). Treating female pattern hair loss. www.harvard.edu › staying-healthy › treating-female-pattern-h.
5. Mayo Clinic Staff. (n.d.). Hair loss. https://www.mayoclinic.org/diseases-conditions/hair-loss. Retrieved 14 Jan. 2022.
6. McAndrews, P.J. (n.d.) Women's hair loss. https://www.americanhairloss.org/women_hair_loss/treatment.html. Retrieved 16 Dec. 2021.
7. *PR Newswire.* (2018, Sept. 4). $10 billion hair wigs and extension market—global outlook and forecast 2018–2023. https://www.prnewswire.com/news-releases/10-billion-hair-wigs-and-extension-market-global-outlook-and-forecast-2018-2023-300706170.html/.
8. *Ibid.*
9. Lane, K. (2020, Dec. 22). This is what it's really like to be Dolly Parton. https://www.thelist.com/300236/this-is-what-its-really-like-to-be-dolly-parton.
10. Garcia, S.E., & Rabin, R.C. (2020,

Jan. 22). Ayanna Pressley opens up about living with alopecia and hair loss. *New York Times.* https://www.nytimes.com/2020/01/16/us/politics/alopecia-ayanna-pressley.html.
11. National Alopecia Areata Foundation. (n.d.). What you need to know about the different types of alopecia. https://www.naaf.org/alopecia-areata/types-of-alopecia-areata. Retrieved 14 Jan. 2022.
12. Press release. (2021, Sept. 30). Pressley, McGovern, colleagues honor Alopecia Areata Awareness Month, unveil bill to support individuals experiencing hair loss. https://pressley.house.gov › media › press-releases › pre.
13. Rachael. (2015, July 16). Wigz on Wheelz makes medical hair loss solutions personal. https://www.hji.co.uk/charity-events/wigz-on-wheelz-makes-medical-hair-loss-solutions-personal/.
14. Farahm, A. (2015, July 8). Everything you've ever wanted to know about wigs—Answered. *Women's Health.* https://www.womenshealthmag.com/beauty/a19981637/wigs/.
15. Minsky, M. (2017, May 4). For Orthodox women, wigs aren't just hair—They're big business. *Marie Claire.* https://www.marieclaire.com/beauty/news/a26982/jewish-orthodox-wig-industry.
16. Gardizy, A. (2021, June 22). "Wigs are the next big thing": A Boston beauty startup wants to make the buying process easier for black women. *Boston Globe.* https://www.bostonglobe.com/2021/06/22/business/wigs-are-next-big-thing-boston-beauty-startup-wants-make-buying-process-easier-black-women/?s_campaign=8315.
17. Report Linker. (2021, Mar.). Hair wigs and extensions market—Global outlook and forecast 2021–2026. https://www.reportlinker.com/p05822878. Retrieved 14 Jan. 2022.
18. Dolgoff, S. (2010). *My formerly hot life: Dispatches from just the other side of young.* Ballantine.
19. Dolgoff, S. (2010, Aug. 3). Personal communication.
20. https://health.clevelandclinic.org/dyeing-your-hair-while-pregnant/
21. https://americanpregnancy.org › healthy-pregnancy ›.

22. Rodgers, J. (2013, Jan. 22). Personal communication.

23. Rogers, J. (2002). *Bald in the land of big hair: A true story.* Harper Perennial.

Chapter 11

1. Ephron 2006, p. 35.

2. Browning, D. (2010, Oct. 21). Why can't middle-aged women have long hair? *New York Times.* https://www.nytimes.com/2010/10/24/fashion/24Mirror.html.

3. Cohen, P. (2009, Mar. 8). Middle age, before it came out of a bottle. *New York Times* https://www.nytimes.com/2009/03/08/weekinreview/08cohen.html.

4. Hoyle, A. (2016, June 14). Women who've NEVER had a single grey hair: They're not fibbing—We asked their hairdressers. *Daily Mail.* https://www.dailymail.co.uk/femail/article-3639887/Women-ve-NEVER-single-grey-hair-not-fibbing-asked.

5. Lowe 2016.

6. Brownmiller 1984, p. 56.

7. Weitz, R. (2004). *Rapunzel's daugters: What women's hair tells us about women's lives.* Farrar, Straus and Giroux.

8. Wood, H. (2019, Sept. 21). 27 hair color statistics, facts & industry trends (that will blow your mind). https://www.holleewoodhair.com/hair-color-statistics/.

9. Cohen 2009.

10. MarketWatch. (2021, Nov. 26). Hair dye market share, size global historical analysis, industry key strategies, segmentation, application, technology, trends and growth opportunities forecasts to 2027. https://www.marketwatch.com/press-release/hair-dye-market-share-size-global-historical-analysis industry-key-strategies-segmentation-application-technology-trends-and-growth-opportunities-forecasts-to-2027-2021-11-26.

11. Wood 2019.

12. Hubbard, L.A. (2018, Dec. 13). Many women are defying the bully: the antiaging industry. Silver Century Foundation. https://www.silvercentury.org/2018/12/many-women...

13. Brooks, A. (2017). *The ways women age: Using and refusing cosmetic intervention.* New York University Press.

14. Hubbard 2018.

15. Davis, L.S. (2021, Sept. 30). TV and movies are finally celebrating older women. *New York Times.* https://www.nytimes.com/2021/09/30/us/tv-movies-hollywood-women.html. (Quote is from Carol Walker, character played by Angela Bassett, in film *Otherhood*.)

16. Federal Reserve Bank of St. Louis. (2015, Nov. 17). Long-term unemployment affected older women most following recession.https://www.stlouisfed.org/on-the-economy/2015/november/older-women-recession-long-term-unemployment.

17. Palmer, K. (2017, Feb. 20). 10 things you should know about age discrimination. AARP. https://www.aarp.org/work/on-the-job/info-2017/age-discrimination-facts.html.

18. Benedict 2015, p. 292.

19. Berg, M.H. (2018, Aug. 25). The great gray-hair debate is one for the ages. *USA Today.* https://www.usatoday.com/story/news/nation/2018/08/25...great-gray-debate/1050835002/.

20. Trasko 1994.

21. Katie. (2021, Dec. 31). Why you should transition to gray hair this year. https://katiegoesplatinum.com/transition-to-gray-hair.

22. Kreamer 2007.

23. https://www.grayisthenewblonde.com.

24. Marie, V. (2021, Feb. 23). Personal communication.

25. Shaw, J. (2021, Sept. 22). Ditched the dye during Covid? Maybe stay gray. *New York Times.* https://www.nytimes.com/2021/09/22/style/gray-hair-women-keep-it.html?smid=em-share. Prinzivalli, L. (2020, Jan. 31). A colorist explains how he created this low-maintenance gray hair transformation. *Allure.* https://www.allure.com/story/colorist-jack-martin-gray-hair-transformation.

26. Engeln 2017.

Chapter 12

1. Simon 2000, p. 230.
2. Krupnick, E. (2013, Feb. 19). Michelle Obama mid-life crisis is the reason for her bangs! *Huffington Post.* https://www.huffpost.com/entry/michelle-obama-mid-life-crisis_n_2715773.
3. www.triciaroseburt.com/bio. Her play *I Will Be Good* is now called *How to Draw a Nekkid Man.*
4. www.youtube.com/watch?v=-l0XZvNip-MM. Accessed 10 Dec. 2021.
5. Burt, T. (2021, Nov. 19). Personal communication.
6. www.fridakahlo.org. (1940). Painting is self portrait with cropped hair.
7. https://www.lyrics.com/lyric/26030561. "I'm Going to Wash That Man Right Outta My Hair."
8. Pantene. (2019, June 19). Pantene: Don't hate me because I'm #BeautifuLGBTQ+. https://campaignsoftheworld.com/tv/pantene-dont-hate-im-beautiful gbtq.
9. McCracken 1995, p. 1.
10. Lowe 2016.

Chapter 13

1. Walker, A. (2013, Sept. 6). Oppressed hair puts a ceiling on the brain. alicewalkersgarden.com/2013/09/oppressed-hair-puts-a-ceiling-on-the-brain.
2. The Crown Coalition. (2019, May 1). New Dove study confirms workplace bias against hairstyles impacts black women's ability to celebrate their natural beauty. https://www.prnewswire.com/news-releases/new-dove-study-confirms-workplace-bias-against-hairstyles-impacts-black-womens-ability-to-celebrate-their-natural-beauty-300842006.html.
3. Dabiri, E. (2019). *Don't touch my hair.* Penguin Random House.
4. Walker 2013.
5. www.youtube.com/watch?v=4ck2o34DS64. Chimamanda Ngozi Adichie: "Hair is political."
6. Adichie, C.N. (2014). *Americanah.* HarperCollins, p. 210.

7. *Good Hair.* (2009). https://www.imdb.com/title/tt1213585.
8. Sesame Street: Song—*I Love My Hair.* https://www.youtube.com/watch?v=enpFde5rgmw.
9. Cherry, M.A. (2019). *Hair Love.* Penguin Random House. https://www.penguinrandomhouse.com/books/585658/hair-love-by-matthew-a-cherry-illustrated-by-vashti-harrison/.
10. http://www.matthewacherry.com/hair-love; https://www.youtube.com/watch?v=936ySvLGxy0.
11. Rice, L. (2019, Dec. 25). The untold truth of Zozibini Tunzi. https://www.stylesrant.com/the-untold-truth-of-zozibini-tunzi.
12. Davis, M.A. (2020, Dec. 6). Our crowns, our glory: America's reigning beauty queens are black, bold and rocking many crowns. *Essence.* https://www.essence com/feature/black-beauty-queens-2019-digital-cove.
13. Davis, V. (2014, Apr. 23). Viola Davis on natural hair. https://going-natural.com/viola-davis-on-natural-hair.
14. Mamona, S. (2020, Oct. 15). This is why black women unfairly spend so much money on their hair. *Glamour.* www.glamourmagazine.co.uk/article/why-black-women-spend-so-much-on-hair.
15. Benjamin, R. (2012, Aug. 8). Surgeon General: Don't let hair get in the way: NPR interview, Michel Martin, host. https://www.npr.org/2012/08/08/158419580.
16. Hall, R.R., Francis, S., Whitt-Glover, M., et al. (2013, Mar.). Hair practices as a barrier to physical activity in African American women. *JAMA Network.* https://jamanetwork.com/journals/jamadermatology/fullarticle/1485354.
17. Qamar, A. (2021, July 2). Black Olympians "disappointed and heartbroken" after ban on swim cap made for natural black hair. *Daily Kos.* https://www.dailykos.com/stories/2021/7/2/2038097/-Black-Olympians-disappointed-and-heartbroken-after-ban-on-s.

Chapter 14

1. *Good Hair.* (2009). https://www.imdb.com/title/tt1213585.

2. Byrd & Tharps 2002.

3. Sherrow 2006.

4. Walker 2013.

5. Lewis, I. (2013). The other n-word: The history and signification of black women's hair in the United States. Honors Thesis African American Studies Department, Emory University. https://etd.library.emory.edu/downloads/3f4625599?locale=de.

6. *Ibid.*

7. Holmes, T.E. (2020, Dec. 6). The industry that black women built. *Essence.* https://www.essence.com/news/money-career/business-black-beauty.

8. Kenneth. (2021, June 7). The natural hair movement: A historical perspective. CurlCentric. https://www.curlcentric.com/natural-hair-movement/.

9. Rhone, N. (2017, Aug. 9). The bald and the beautiful: Black women need to get real about hair weaves. *The Atlanta Journal-Constitution.* https://www.ajc.com/blog/talk-town/the-bald-and-the-beautiful-black-women-need-get-real-about-hair-weaves/idOP7lJNwecQaUMfAG0RUO/.

10. Johns Hopkins Medicine. (2016, Apr. 27). All hairstyles are not created equal. http://www.hopkinsmedicine.org/news/media/releases/all_hairstyles_are_not_created_equal.

11. Greene, H.F. (2011, May 11). What spending a half a trillion dollars on hair care and weaves says about us. *Madamenoire.* http://madamenoire.com/57134/what-spending-a-half-a-trillion-dollars-on-hair-care-and-weaves-says-about-us/4/.

12. Harmon, S. (2018, Feb. 26). Black consumers spend nine times more in hair & beauty: Report. https://www.hypehair.com/86642/black-consumers-continue-to-spend-nine-times-more-in-beauty-report/.

13. Vesper, I. (2018, May 11). Hair products popular with black women may contain harmful chemicals. *Scientific American.* https://www.scientificamerican.com/article/hair-products-popular-with-black-women-may-contain-harmful.

14. *Ibid.*

15. www.Nappturality.com.

16. Thompson, C. (2009). Black women and identity: What's hair got to do with it? *Michigan Feminist Studies, 22,* Fall, 78–79. https://quod.lib.umich.edu/m/mfsfront/ark5583.0022.

17. National Legal Defense and Education Fund. (2022). https://www.naacpldf.org/natural-hair-discrimination. Retrieved 14 Jan. 2022.

18. Gandy, I. (2018, May 6). The U.S. Supreme Court decided to ignore black hair discrimination. *Rewire News Group.* https://rewirenewsgroup.com/ablc/2018/05/16/u-s-supreme-court-ignoring-black-hair-discrimination/.

19. Lazar, K. (2017, May 11). Black Malden charter students punished for braided hair extensions. *Boston Globe.* https://www.bostonglobe.com/metro/2017/05/11/black-students-malden-school-who-wear-braids-face-punishment-parents-say/stWDlBSCJhw1zocUWR1QMP/story.html.

20. Almasy, S., & Holcombe, M. (2019, Sept. 19). Referee in dreadlock haircut controversy has been suspended for two years. CNN.com. https://edition.cnn.com/2019/09/19/us/new-jersey.

21. McLaughlin, K. (2020, Jan. 23). A black teen was told he couldn't walk in his upcoming graduation unless he cuts his dreadlocks. *Insider.com.* https://www.insider.com/texas-student-cut-dreadlocks-graduation-ban-2020-1-23.

22. Shepherd, K. (2020, Jan. 30). Do the right thing: Ellen DeGeneres pleads for school to let black teen with dreadlocks walk at graduation. *Washington Post.* https://www.washingtonpost.com/nation/2020/01/30/ellen-arnold-dreadlocks.

23. Keating, C. (2021, Mar. 2). Connecticut Senate votes to ban hair discrimination. *Hartford Courant.* https://www.courant.com/politics/capitol-watch/hc-pol-crown-act-hair-discrimination-20210302-bdv2oxkw7nfvrjygyrd6fv4vuy-story.html.

24. www.thecrownact.com.

25. Stowe, S. (2019, Feb. 18). New York City to ban discrimination based on hair. *New York Times.* https://www.nytimes.com/2019/02/18/style/hair-discrimination-new-york-city.html.

26. Salvadore, S. (2020, Feb. 2). Catholic schools slow to accept cultural significance of black hair. *National Catholic Reporter.* https://www.ncronline.org/news/justice/catholic-schools-slow-accept-cultural-significance-black-hair.

27. Evans, C. (2012, Feb. 21). Relaxers and fibroids? Blackdoctor.org. https://blackdoctor.org/do-relaxers-cause-fibroids/. For more info on these health related connections visit www.blackdoctor.org.

28. Moe. (2007, Aug. 14). Glamour editor to lady lawyers being black is kinda a corporate don't. *Jezebel.* http://jezebel.com/289268/glamour-editor-to-lady-lawyers-being-black-is-kinda-a-corporate-dont.

29. Banks, I. (2000). *Hair matters: Beauty, power, and black woman's consciousness.* New York University Press.

Chapter 15

1. Bollick, K. (2019). *Masters at work: Becoming a hairstylist.* Simon & Schuster, p. 20.

2. U.S. Bureau of Labor Statistics. (2021, Sept .8). *Barbers, hairstylists, and cosmetologists: Occupational outlook handbook.* https://www.bls.gov/ooh/personal-care-and-service/barbers-hairstylists-and-cosmetologists.htm.

3. Educational Roadmaps by Career. (n.d.). 5 steps to becoming a professional hair stylist. Learn.org. https://learn.org/articles/Hair_Stylist_5_Steps_to_Becoming_a_Professional_Hair_Stylist.html. Retrieved 15 Jan. 2022.

4. Alhamed, A. (2018, Jan. 16). Is being a hairstylist as low-stress job? *Modern Salon.* https://www.modernsalon.com/376145/is-being-a-hairstylist-a-low-stress-job.

5. Pottell, N. (2016, Jan. 25). We hairdressers can be therapists and magicians, too. No wonder people trust us. *The Guardian.*www.theguardian.com/commentisfree/2016/jan/25/hairdressers-people-trust-profession-mps.

6. Sherrow 2006.

7. Stenn 2016.

8. Hair Salon in the U.S. Industry Statistics (2021, May 11). *IBIS World.* https://www.ibisworld.com/united-states/market-research-reports/hair-salons-industry/.

9. Willett, J.A. (2000). *Permanent waves: The making of the American beauty shop.* New York: New York University Press.

10. DiDonato, J. (2020, Mar. 9). Separate but not equal: Racial bias in salon culture. *Huffington Post.* https://www.huffpost.com/entry/racial-bias-salons-black-hair_l_5e5d45fec5b63aaf8f5b199d.

11. *Ibid.*

12. Levy, L. (2018, June 18). Millennial hair stylists don't get references to Buster Brown or Mamie Eisenhower. https://midcenturymodernmag.com/bad-hair-day-2b9673bdb3e4.

13. www.urbandictionary.com › define › term=hairapy. Accessed 29 Oct. 2021.

14. Blomsterberg, M. (2006). *Hairapy: Deeper than the roots.* Los Angeles: MLR Publishing.

15. Fripp, P. (2020, 7 Sept. 2010). Personal communication.

16. MailOnline Reporter (2014, Sept. 26). Hate your haircut? You're not alone—one in five American women has left a salon in tears at least once in their life. *Daily Mail.* https://www.dailymail.co.uk/femail/article-2770859.

17. https://en.wikipedia.org/wiki/Desairology:_Funeral_Cosmetology.

18. Giles, C. (2020, Mar. 17). A Baltimore barber who's with his clients through life and death. *New York Times.* https://www.nytimes.com/2020/03/17/us/baltimore-barber-gun-violence.html.

19. Rodriguez, D. (2013, Apr. 8). Personal communication.

20. Rodriguez, D. (2007). *Kabul Beauty School: An American woman goes Behind the veil.* New York: Random House.

21. Mondays at Racine. https://www.mondaysatracine.org. Retrieved 15 Jan. 2022.

22. Cut Out Cancer at Milano—Connecticut. http://cutoutcancerct.org/ Retrieved 15 Jan. 2022. cutoutcancerct.org.

23. https://www.wigsandwishes.org/ Retrieved 15 Jan. 2022.

24. https://www.probeauty.org/pba-charities/cio/charities. Retrieved 15 Jan. 2022.

Conclusion

1. Lowe 2016, p. 125.

Appendix

1. Gibran, K. (1923). *The Prophet.* Knopf, p. 35.
2. For more about Beginner's Mind, see https://jackkornfield.com/beginners-mind/.
3. Rico, G. (2000). *Writing the natural way: Using right-brain techniques to release your expressive powers* (2nd rev. ed.). Tarcher Putnam, pp. 16–23.
4. Adrienne Ressler is a specialist in body image and eating disorders and vice president of professional development at The Renfrew Center Foundation. This exercise is a variation of one she uses in group therapy settings or professional training. Personal communication 7 Dec. 2021.

Bibliography

Adichie, C.N. (2014). *Americanah*. Harper-Collins.

Alinejad, M. (2018). *The wind in my hair*. Little, Brown.

Banks, I. (2000). *Hair matters: Beauty, power, and Black woman's consciousness*. New York University Press.

Barak-Brandes, S., & Kama, A. (Eds.). (2018). *Feminist interrogations of women's head hair: Crown of glory and shame*. Routledge, 2018.

Benedict, E. (Ed.). (2015). *Me, my hair, and I: 27 women untangle an obsession*. Algonquin Books of Chapel Hill.

Brooks, A. (2017). *The ways women age: Using and refusing cosmetic intervention*. New York University Press.

Brownmiller, S. (1984). *Femininity*. Fawcett Columbine.

Byrd, A.D., & Tharps, L. (2002). *Hair story: Untangling the roots of Black hair in America*. St. Martin's.

Cash, T.F., & Smolak, L. (2011). *Body image: A handbook of science, practice, and prevention*, 2nd ed. Guilford Press.

Cherry, M.A. (2019). *Hair love*. Penguin Random House.

Corson, R. (2005). *Fashions in hair: The first five thousand years*. Peter Owens.

Dabri, E. (2019). *Don't touch my hair*. Penguin Random House.

Eliberg-Schwartz, H., & Doniger, W. (Eds.). *Off with her head! The denial of women's identity in myth, religion, and culture*. University of California Press.

Engeln, R. (2017). *Beauty sick: How the cultural obsession with appearance hurts girls and women*. Harper.

Ephron, N. (2006). *I feel bad about my neck: And other thoughts on being a woman*. Vintage.

Etcoff, N. (2000). *Survival of the prettiest: The science of beauty*. Anchor.

Gill, T.M. (2010). *Beauty shop politics: African American women's activism in the beauty industry (Women, gender, and sexuality in American history)*. University of Illinois Press.

Jacobs-Huey, L. (2006). *From the kitchen to the parlor: Language and becoming in African American women's hair care (Studies in language and gender, first edition)*. Oxford University Press.

Johnson, E. (2016). *Resistance and empowerment in black women's styling: Interdisciplinary research series in ethnic, gender and class*. Routledge.

Kreamer, A. (2007). *Going gray: How to embrace your authentic self with grace and style*. Little, Brown.

Lowe, S. (2016). *Object lessons: Hair*. Bloomsbury Academic.

Massey, L., & Chiel, D. (2011). *Curly girl: The handbook*. Workman.

McCracken, G. (1995). *Big hair: A journey into the transformation of self*. The Overlook Press.

Mensah, C. (2020). *Good hair: The essential guide to Afro, textured and curly hair*. Penguin.

'Okhai Ojeikere, J.D. (2000). *Photographs*. Scalo.

Rhode, D. (2010). *The beauty bias: The injustice of appearance in life and law*. Oxford University Press.

Rodriguez, D. (2007). *Kabul beauty school: An American woman goes behind the veil*. Random House.

Rogers, J. (2002). *Bald in the land of big hair: A true story*. Harper Perennial.

Scheper-Hughes, N., & Lock, M. (1987). The mindful body: A prolegomenon

Bibliography

to future work in medical anthropology. *Medical Anthropology Quarterly* 1: 6–41.

Sherrow, V. (2006). *Encyclopedia of hair: A cultural history.* Greenwood Press.

Simon, D. (2000). *Hair: Public, political, extremely personal.* Thomas Dunne.

Stenn, K. (2016). *Hair: A human history.* Pegasus.

Sullivan, L., & Deslauriers, L. (2016). *Awakening hair: Caring for your cosmic antenna.* Sundream.

Tannen, D. (2006). *You're wearing that? Understanding mothers and daughters in conversation.* Random House.

Tarlo, E. (2016). *Entanglement: The secret lives of hair.* One World.

Thompson, C. (2009). Black women and identity: What's hair got to do with it? *Michigan Feminist Studies, 22,* Fall, 78–79. https://quod.lib.umich.edu/m/mfsfront/ark5583.0022.

Trasko, M. (1994). *Daring do's: A history of extraordinary hair.* Flammarion.

Walker, A. (1989). *Living by the word: Selected writings, 1973–1987.* Amistad.

Weitz, R. (2004). *Rapunzel's daughters: What women's hair tells us about women's lives.* Farrar, Straus & Giroux.

Willett, J.A. (2000). *Permanent Waves: The making of the American beauty shop.* New York University Press.

Index

Index

body record, hair as 30–31
body self 3, 11, 23
Bollick, Kate 153
Brahmin women 31
Brooks, Abigail 109
brown hair color 17, 21, 40, 69–70, 84–85, 88
Browning, Dominique 105
Brownmiller, Susan 40, 56, 107
Buddhist monks 38
bulimia nervosa 16
Burt, Tricia Rose 119

cancer 39, 78, 81, 90, 93, 96, 100–103, 115, 123, 126, 145, 165–167
career 20, 44, 52, 54, 66, 102, 110, 115, 119, 121, 148, 154, 165
Catholicism 12, 150–151, 156
celebrity hair 30, 50, 94
Chanel, CoCo 13
chemical toxicity/risk 20, 31, 58, 79, 96, 115, 145
Cherry, Matthew 133
Cheveux Cheris (Lovely Hair; 2013 Musée Quai Branly exhibit) 33
children 18, 20, 30, 36, 39, 49, 53, 76, 79, 99–102, 106, 111, 125, 140, 144–146, 167, 175
Clairol *"Does she or doesn't she?"* ad campaign 108
Clinton, Hillary Rodham 22–3
code, hair as 13, 33, 51
coming of age rituals 31, 34, 36, 38, 47
coming out 120
conditioners 29, 35, 86
confidantes: barbers as 28; stylists as 28, 77, 67, 93, 153–164, 166, 168, 172, 192
Conscious Hair-Raising 79–80
Constraint and Control 12, 51
COVID-19 pandemic 110, 113,116, 119, 153
Crawford, Joan (Lucille Fay LeSueur) 157
CROWN ACT (Create a Respectful and Open Workplace for Natural Hair) 149–150
Crown Chakra 5
culture 1, 11–13, 20–21, 34, 38, 39, 48, 50, 53, 73, 79, 83, 86–87, 99, 106,

108–109, 111, 114, 122, 124, 126, 130, 132, 135, 138, 141–142, 144, 146, 149–151, 156, 171
Cut It Out (Professional Beauty Association domestic violence program) 167–168
Cut Out Cancer @ Milano 167

Davis, Michaela Angela 135
DeGeneres, Ellen 148
Delaney, Carol PhD 48
despair 14–15, 17–18, 46
detanglers 29
dieting 82
discrimination 130, 132, 135, 138, 141–142, 144, 146, 149–151, 156; and age 51, 109–111, 113; *see also* grooming policies as condition of employment
Disney princesses 40, 124
divorce 17, 20, 32, 47, 97, 99, 119–120, 127
DNA 1, 31
Dolgoff, Stephanie 94
Douglas, William O. (US Supreme Court Justice) 51
Dow, Antoine 164–165
dream imagery, hair in 28, 58
dress code 148
dye for hair 51, 105, 107, 109, 113, 119

eating disorders 1, 3, 5, 7, 14, 90, 103–104
Egypt 35–36
emotion 5, 12–16, 18, 31, 142, 115, 118, 127, 135, 144, 153, 156, 162, 167–168, 170
endocrine disruptors 145
Engeln, Renee PhD 184
enslavement/slavery 34, 36, 57, 141–142, 138
Ephron, Nora 54, 74, 105
Equal Employment Opportunity Commission (EEOC) 147
essential workers, stylists as 153–161
Ethiopia 133
Eurocentric beauty standards 134, 142, 147, 150
exercise 105, 135, 138–140

Index

Index

Wharton, Edith (Edith Newbold Jones) 52
White, C. Vanessa 151
wigs 13, 16, 21, 30, 36–37, 39, 47, 56, 76–78, 85, 88–89, 91–94, 98, 112, 120, 123, 134, 137, 143, 146, 167, 177–178
Wigs & Wishes (charity) 167
Wigz on Wheels 93

Winfrey, Oprah 55, 56
workplace 20, 42, 45, 51, 107, 111, 114, 122, 130, 149–150, 152

youth 14, 20, 31, 40, 55, 70, 72, 76, 78, 80, 83, 94, 100, 107, 109, 111–112, 115, 124–125, 128, 131, 144, 148, 164, 172, 175